WHAT ON EARTH IS HAPPENING?

Discovery House Publishers

Books, music, and videos that feed the soul with the Word of God

Box 3566 Grand Rapids, MI 49501

WHAT ON EARTH IS HAPPENING?

What JESUS Said About the End of the Age

RAY STEDMAN
EDITED BY JAMES DENNEY

What on Earth Is Happening?
What Jesus Said About the End of the Age
© 2003 by Elaine Stedman

Discovery House Publishers is affiliated with RBC Ministries,
Grand Rapids, Michigan 49512.
All rights reserved.
Discovery House books are distributed to the trade exclusively by
Barbour Publishing, Inc., Uhrichsville, Ohio 44683.

.

Interior design by Sherri L. Hoffman

Library of Congress Cataloging-in-Publication Data
Stedman, Ray C.
What on earth is happening? : what Jesus said about the end of the
    Age / by Ray C. Stedman.
    p.   cm.
    ISBN 1-57293-092-6
1. Jesus Christ—Teachings. 2. Eschatology—Biblical teaching. 3. Bible.
    N.T. Matthew XXIV-XXV—Commentaries. I. Title.
BS2417.E7S74 2003
226.2'077—dc21   2003003908

Printed in the United States of America
03 04 05 06 07 08 09 / / 10 9 8 7 6 5 4 3 2 1

Contents

Editors' Preface

———

Ray Stedman (1917–1992) pastored the Peninsula Bible Church from 1950 to 1990, where he was known and loved as a man of outstanding Bible knowledge and wisdom coupled with a depth of Christian integrity, love, and humility. Born in Temvik, North Dakota, Ray grew up on the rugged landscape of Montana. When he was a small child, his mother became ill and his father, a railroad man, abandoned the family, so Ray grew up on his aunt's Montana farm from the time he was six. He came to know the Lord at a Methodist revival meeting at age ten. Ray immediately felt called by God to preach and would often go out to the pasture and preach to the cows.

As a young man he tried his hand at different jobs, working in Chicago, Denver, Hawaii, and elsewhere. He enlisted in the Navy during World War II while in Hawaii, where he often led Bible studies for civilians and Navy personnel, and even preached on local radio. At the close of the war, Ray was married in Honolulu, though he and his wife Elaine had first met in Great Falls, Montana. They returned to the mainland in 1946, and Ray graduated from Dallas Theological Seminary in 1950. After two seminary summers interning under the widely regarded Bible teacher, Dr. J. Vernon McGee, Ray traveled for several months with another renowned theologian, Dr. H. A. Ironside, pastor of Moody Church in Chicago.

In 1950, Ray was called by the two-year-old Peninsula Bible Fellowship in Palo Alto, California, to serve as its first pastor. That new and thriving ministry later became Peninsula Bible Church, where Ray eventually served a forty-year tenure, retiring on April 30, 1990. During those years, Ray Stedman authored a number of life-changing Christian books, including the classic work on the meaning and mission of the church, *Body Life*.

The book you hold in your hands is the product of Ray's careful study of the Olivet discourse of Jesus, found in Matthew 24–25 as well as in Mark 13 and Luke 21. Here we find the Lord's own description of the end of history—a description that dovetails with other prophetic passages of Scripture, from the Old Testament prophecy of Daniel to the New Testament Revelation of the apostle John. In light of current events in the Middle East and heightened interest in Bible prophecy throughout our society, we believe the message in this book has never been more timely and relevant.

Before he passed away in 1992, Ray Stedman left this book, now published for the first time, eleven years after his death. Unlike so many books that sensationalize the subject, *What on Earth Is Happening?* is a sober, rational, thoughtful approach to Bible prophecy. It is not a lofty theological treatise but a readable, friendly conversation. Although the subject matter is serious, Ray's warmth and humor make this an enjoyable and comforting book to read.

In these pages, you will discover the future as Jesus first unveiled it to His disciples on the Mount of Olives two thousand years ago. We believe this book will do more than inform you about the future. It will change your life right here, right now. So settle back, turn the page, and begin your journey.

The future begins now.

— The Editors

The Text of the Olivet Discourse

Matthew 24 and 25 (NIV)

Matthew 24

¹ Jesus left the temple and was walking away when his disciples came up to him to call his attention to its buildings. ² "Do you see all these things?" he asked. "I tell you the truth, not one stone here will be left on another; every one will be thrown down."

³ As Jesus was sitting on the Mount of Olives, the disciples came to him privately. "Tell us," they said, "when will this happen, and what will be the sign of your coming and of the end of the age?"

⁴ Jesus answered: "Watch out that no one deceives you. ⁵ For many will come in my name, claiming, 'I am the Christ,' and will deceive many. ⁶ You will hear of wars and rumors of wars, but see to it that you are not alarmed. Such things must happen, but the end is still to come. ⁷ Nation will rise against nation, and kingdom against kingdom. There will be famines and earthquakes in various places. ⁸ All these are the beginning of birth pains.

⁹ "Then you will be handed over to be persecuted and put to death, and you will be hated by all nations because of me. ¹⁰ At that time many will turn away from the faith and will betray and hate each other, ¹¹ and many false prophets will appear and deceive many people. ¹² Because of the increase of wickedness, the love of most will grow cold, ¹³ but he who stands firm to the end will be saved. ¹⁴ And this

gospel of the kingdom will be preached in the whole world as a testimony to all nations, and then the end will come.

[15] "So when you see standing in the holy place 'the abomination that causes desolation,' spoken of through the prophet Daniel—let the reader understand— [16] then let those who are in Judea flee to the mountains. [17] Let no one on the roof of his house go down to take anything out of the house. [18] Let no one in the field go back to get his cloak. [19] How dreadful it will be in those days for pregnant women and nursing mothers! [20] Pray that your flight will not take place in winter or on the Sabbath. [21] For then there will be great distress, unequaled from the beginning of the world until now—and never to be equaled again. [22] If those days had not been cut short, no one would survive, but for the sake of the elect those days will be shortened. [23] At that time if anyone says to you, 'Look, here is the Christ!' or, 'There he is!' do not believe it. [24] For false Christs and false prophets will appear and perform great signs and miracles to deceive even the elect—if that were possible. [25] See, I have told you ahead of time.

[26] "So if anyone tells you, 'There he is, out in the desert,' do not go out; or, 'Here he is, in the inner rooms,' do not believe it. [27] For as lightning that comes from the east is visible even in the west, so will be the coming of the Son of Man. [28] Wherever there is a carcass, there the vultures will gather.

[29] "Immediately after the distress of those days

> " 'the sun will be darkened,
>   and the moon will not give its light;
> the stars will fall from the sky,
>   and the heavenly bodies will be shaken.'

[30] "At that time the sign of the Son of Man will appear in the sky, and all the nations of the earth will mourn. They will see the Son of Man coming on the clouds of the sky, with power and great glory. [31] And he will send his angels with a loud trumpet call, and they will gather his elect from the four winds, from one end of the heavens to the other.

[32] "Now learn this lesson from the fig tree: As soon as its twigs get tender and its leaves come out, you know that summer is near. [33] Even so, when you see all these things, you know that it is near, right at the door. [34] I tell you the truth, this generation will certainly not pass away until all these things have happened. [35] Heaven and earth will pass away, but my words will never pass away.

[36] "No one knows about that day or hour, not even the angels in heaven, nor the Son, but only the Father. [37] As it was in the days of Noah, so it will be at the coming of the Son of Man. [38] For in the days before the flood, people were eating and drinking, marrying and giving in marriage, up to the day Noah entered the ark; [39] and they knew nothing about what would happen until the flood came and took them all away. That is how it will be at the coming of the Son of Man. [40] Two men will be in the field; one will be taken and the other left. [41] Two women will be grinding with a hand mill; one will be taken and the other left.

[42] "Therefore keep watch, because you do not know on what day your Lord will come. [43] But understand this: If the owner of the house had known at what time of night the thief was coming, he would have kept watch and would not have let his house be broken into. [44] So you also must be ready, because the Son of Man will come at an hour when you do not expect him.

[45] "Who then is the faithful and wise servant, whom the master has put in charge of the servants in his household to give them their food at the proper time? [46] It will be good for that servant whose master finds him doing so when he returns. [47] I tell you the truth, he will put him in charge of all his possessions. [48] But suppose that servant is wicked and says to himself, 'My master is staying away a long time,' [49] and he then begins to beat his fellow servants and to eat and drink with drunkards. [50] The master of that servant will come on a day when he does not expect him and at an hour he is not aware of. [51] He will cut him to pieces and assign him a place with the hypocrites, where there will be weeping and gnashing of teeth.

Matthew 25

[1] "At that time the kingdom of heaven will be like ten virgins who took their lamps and went out to meet the bridegroom. [2] Five of them were foolish and five were wise. [3] The foolish ones took their lamps but did not take any oil with them. [4] The wise, however, took oil in jars along with their lamps. [5] The bridegroom was a long time in coming, and they all became drowsy and fell asleep.

[6] "At midnight the cry rang out: 'Here's the bridegroom! Come out to meet him!'

[7] "Then all the virgins woke up and trimmed their lamps. [8] The foolish ones said to the wise, 'Give us some of your oil; our lamps are going out.'

[9] "'No,' they replied, 'there may not be enough for both us and you. Instead, go to those who sell oil and buy some for yourselves.'

[10] "But while they were on their way to buy the oil, the bridegroom arrived. The virgins who were ready went in with him to the wedding banquet. And the door was shut.

[11] "Later the others also came. 'Sir! Sir!' they said. 'Open the door for us!'

[12] "But he replied, 'I tell you the truth, I don't know you.'

[13] "Therefore keep watch, because you do not know the day or the hour.

[14] "Again, it will be like a man going on a journey, who called his servants and entrusted his property to them. [15] To one he gave five talents of money, to another two talents, and to another one talent, each according to his ability. Then he went on his journey. [16] The man who had received the five talents went at once and put his money to work and gained five more. [17] So also, the one with the two talents gained two more. [18] But the man who had received the one talent went off, dug a hole in the ground and hid his master's money.

[19] "After a long time the master of those servants returned and settled accounts with them. [20] The man who had received the five talents

brought the other five. 'Master,' he said, 'you entrusted me with five talents. See, I have gained five more.'

[21] "His master replied, 'Well done, good and faithful servant! You have been faithful with a few things; I will put you in charge of many things. Come and share your master's happiness!'

[22] "The man with the two talents also came. 'Master,' he said, 'you entrusted me with two talents; see, I have gained two more.'

[23] "His master replied, 'Well done, good and faithful servant! You have been faithful with a few things; I will put you in charge of many things. Come and share your master's happiness!'

[24] "Then the man who had received the one talent came. 'Master,' he said, 'I knew that you are a hard man, harvesting where you have not sown and gathering where you have not scattered seed. [25] So I was afraid and went out and hid your talent in the ground. See, here is what belongs to you.'

[26] "His master replied, 'You wicked, lazy servant! So you knew that I harvest where I have not sown and gather where I have not scattered seed? [27] Well then, you should have put my money on deposit with the bankers, so that when I returned I would have received it back with interest.

[28] "'Take the talent from him and give it to the one who has the ten talents. [29] For everyone who has will be given more, and he will have an abundance. Whoever does not have, even what he has will be taken from him. [30] And throw that worthless servant outside, into the darkness, where there will be weeping and gnashing of teeth.'

[31] "When the Son of Man comes in his glory, and all the angels with him, he will sit on his throne in heavenly glory. [32] All the nations will be gathered before him, and he will separate the people one from another as a shepherd separates the sheep from the goats. [33] He will put the sheep on his right and the goats on his left.

[34] "Then the King will say to those on his right, 'Come, you who are blessed by my Father; take your inheritance, the kingdom prepared for you since the creation of the world. [35] For I was hungry and you

gave me something to eat, I was thirsty and you gave me something to drink, I was a stranger and you invited me in, [36] I needed clothes and you clothed me, I was sick and you looked after me, I was in prison and you came to visit me.'

[37] "Then the righteous will answer him, 'Lord, when did we see you hungry and feed you, or thirsty and give you something to drink? [38] When did we see you a stranger and invite you in, or needing clothes and clothe you? [39] When did we see you sick or in prison and go to visit you?'

[40] "The King will reply, 'I tell you the truth, whatever you did for one of the least of these brothers of mine, you did for me.'

[41] "Then he will say to those on his left, 'Depart from me, you who are cursed, into the eternal fire prepared for the devil and his angels. [42] For I was hungry and you gave me nothing to eat, I was thirsty and you gave me nothing to drink, [43] I was a stranger and you did not invite me in, I needed clothes and you did not clothe me, I was sick and in prison and you did not look after me.'

[44] "They also will answer, 'Lord, when did we see you hungry or thirsty or a stranger or needing clothes or sick or in prison, and did not help you?'

[45] "He will reply, 'I tell you the truth, whatever you did not do for one of the least of these, you did not do for me.'

[46] "Then they will go away to eternal punishment, but the righteous to eternal life."

1

The Long Look Ahead

Matthew 24:1–3

In 1870, a bishop came to an Indiana college campus for a denominational conference. During his visit, the bishop heard the president of the college say something that shocked him. "We live in an age of wonders," said the head of the college. "I believe the day is not far off when men will fly in the skies like birds."

"Sir," the bishop said, "you are speaking blasphemy! The Bible tells us that the gift of flight is reserved strictly for the angels!"

Ironically, that bishop's name was Milton Wright. Only three decades after he spoke those words, Bishop Wright's two sons, Wilbur and Orville Wright, made the first successful heavier-than-air flight from a windy hill at Kitty Hawk, North Carolina.

Before judging Bishop Wright too harshly, we should ask ourselves: Are our powers of prediction any better than his? The fact is, when it comes to forecasting the future, some of the best and brightest minds have had very cloudy "crystal balls." A few examples:

In 1899, Charles H. Duell, Director of the U. S. Patent Office, assured President McKinley, "Everything that can be invented has already been invented."

In 1903, the president of the Michigan Savings Bank denied a loan to a young car-building entrepreneur named Henry Ford. The banker told Ford, "The horse is here to stay, and the automobile is only a novelty—a passing fad."

In 1921, a *New York Times* editorial ridiculed rocket pioneer Robert Goddard, who predicted that human beings would eventually explore space in rocket-powered vehicles. "Professor Goddard," said the *Times*, "does not know the relation between action and reaction and the need to have something better than a vacuum against which to react. He seems to lack the basic knowledge ladled out daily in high schools." In July 1969—less than five decades later—the same newspaper used its largest headline type to announce MEN WALK ON MOON. Inside the paper, the newspaper printed a retraction of the 1921 editorial.

In 1949, *Popular Mechanics* predicted, "Computers in the future may weigh no more than 1.5 tons." By the end of the century, mass-produced computers, thousands of times more powerful than those envisioned in 1949, could fit in the palm of your hand.

In 1954, the manager of Nashville's Grand Ole Opry told a young singer, "You ain't goin' nowhere, son. You'd best stick to drivin' trucks." The singer's name was Elvis Presley.

In 1962, the Decca Recording Company turned down a mop-haired rock-and-roll quartet, saying, "We don't like their sound, and besides, guitar music is on the way out." The band they rejected was The Beatles.

Foretelling the future is a risky undertaking—unless you have the ability to see the future with absolute clarity. Who has that ability? Only God! In Isaiah 46:9–11, He says, "I am God, and there is no other; I am God, and there is none like me. I make known the end from the beginning, from ancient times, what is still to come. I say: My purpose will stand, and I will do all that I please. From the east I summon a bird of prey; from a far-off land, a man to fulfill my purpose. What I have said, that will I bring about; what I have planned, that will I do."

Some people claim to have power to predict the future. But if you closely examine their "predictions," you find their forecasts either riddled with error or so vague as to be meaningless. But God's predictions are neither vague nor faulty. Why? Because He has a power that far surpasses that of mere human beings: He not only sees the future, He ordains it and brings events to pass.

Wouldn't you like to know the future? If it were possible, wouldn't you like to lift the curtain of tomorrow and read the future as if it were a history book? Well, there truly is a Book of future history. Unlike the mystics and psychics with their fuzzy hit-or-miss "prophecies," the great Book of future history, the Bible, has a batting average of 1.000. Many of its prophecies have already been fulfilled with astounding precision and reliability. The rest are either being fulfilled right now in our newspaper headlines, or they await an inevitable fulfillment in a certain future.

Most books do well if they are merely "up-to-date." But the Bible isn't just up-to-date—it's ahead of its time!

The Olivet Prophecy:
The Most Detailed Prediction in the Bible

There are many predictive passages in both the Old and New Testaments, but none is clearer or more detailed than the message Jesus delivered from the Mount of Olives. This message was given during the turbulent events of the Lord's last week before the cross.

Olivet, or the Mount of Olives, is a ridge to the east of Jerusalem overlooking the city. In the Old Testament, Olivet was the place where King David fled to escape the murderous conspiracy of his scheming son, Absalom (2 Samuel 15:30), and the place where Ezekiel saw the glory of the Lord (Ezekiel 11:23). It is also the place where the Messiah will stand against the horde of nations that come to attack Jerusalem (Zechariah 14:4). Olivet is the place Jesus often went for rest and refuge; it was also the site of His ascension (Acts 1:12). The towns of Bethany and Bethphage are located high on the eastern side of Olivet, and the Garden of Gethsemane is situated on its lower western slope.

A *discourse* is a lengthy discussion on a single topic. The topic of the Olivet discourse is a theme that continues to fascinate us today: the ultimate fate of Earth. From that crucial point in time, Jesus looked forward and predicted the destruction of the city of Jerusalem (AD 70) and the social upheaval connected with that event. Then He looked beyond, across the centuries, and outlined the perils of that period between His first and Second Coming— the age in which we live.

Then He looked past the present day to a time called "the end of the age," and He set the events of that age before us in searing and vivid detail. His prophecy of the end of the age culminates in His own return to earth and the dawn of a new day.

The Olivet discourse of Jesus is found in three parallel accounts: Matthew 24–25, Mark 13, and Luke 21. We will use the Matthew account as our primary text of the Olivet discourse, while drawing upon the parallel accounts as necessary. We will also take side trips to the remarkable Old Testament prophecy of Daniel and the New Testament prophecy of the book of Revelation. In fact, the Olivet prophecy of Jesus is the key that unlocks the true meaning of Daniel and Revelation—two prophecies that also describe many of these same "end of the age" events.

As we read this astonishing prophecy of Jesus, we will discover that the future He predicts is nothing more or less than the unfolding of events from trends that are already at work in human society. The future has already begun. Even as you read these words, we are living out the prophecy that the Lord outlined for us on that Judean mountainside shortly before His crucifixion. As we study the Olivet prophecy, we will not only have a deeper understanding of the future, we will have a more complete understanding of the events taking place around us in our own day.

Leaving the Temple

This amazing prophetic message is introduced to us in the opening verses of Matthew 24. These three verses give us the key to the structure of Jesus' prophecy and the outline of future events:

> Jesus left the temple and was walking away when his disciples came up to him to call his attention to its buildings. "Do you see all these things?" he asked. "I tell you the truth, not one stone here will be left on another; every one will be thrown down."
>
> As Jesus was sitting on the Mount of Olives, the disciples came to him privately. "Tell us," they said, "when will this happen, and what will be the sign of your coming and of the end of the age?" (Matthew 24:1–3)

Isn't it strange that the disciples came to Jesus and pointed out to Him the beauty of the temple buildings? He had often been with the disciples in the temple area, teaching in those same temple courts. So why were they suddenly interested in pointing out the temple buildings to Him?

This incident grows out of the astonishment the disciples felt at the recent actions of the Lord. The chapter opens with the significant phrase, "Jesus left the temple." It is important to realize what a profound statement that is. He didn't just walk out of a building. He left the temple—and He would never enter the temple again. He left after having pronounced a sentence of judgment upon the temple and the corrupt "worship" conducted there:

> "O Jerusalem, Jerusalem, you who kill the prophets and stone those sent to you, how often I have longed to gather your children together, as a hen gathers her chicks under her wings, but you were not willing. Look, your house is left to you desolate. For I tell you, you will not see me again until you say, 'Blessed is he who comes in the name of the Lord.'" (Matthew 23:37–39)

This comes at the close of the most blistering sermon Jesus ever delivered. That sermon, addressed to the scribes and the Pharisees, consisted of a series of "woes" pronounced upon the hypocrisy of these religious leaders. They were supposed to be the teachers of the people but were actually hindering them from knowing the truth of God. Having begun His ministry with a series of eight blessings (the Beatitudes, recorded in Matthew 5), Jesus closed His ministry with a series of eight woes.

Nothing arouses more vehement anger in the heart of God than self-righteous religious hypocrisy. Throughout the Scriptures, God's most scorching terms are reserved for those who profess to know Him but whose behavior betrays and belies their profession of "faith."

Cleansing the Temple

Many people do not realize that Jesus cleansed the temple in Jerusalem twice. The first cleansing of the temple is recorded in John

2:13–21, where John tells us that Jesus drove the money changers from His Father's house at the beginning of His public ministry. The second cleansing of the temple took place three years later and is recorded in Mark 11:12–19. It cannot be the same event that John mentions, for this cleansing of the temple takes place near the end of His public ministry, shortly before the Crucifixion.

In the case of the second cleansing, Jesus went to Jerusalem during His final week on earth and began to drive out all of those who bought and sold in the temple area. In this account, Mark records a significant action of Jesus that is often overlooked. Note the words I have inserted in brackets in this passage from Mark 11:

> On reaching Jerusalem, Jesus entered the temple area and began driving out those who were buying and selling there. He overturned the tables of the money changers and the benches of those selling doves, and would not allow anyone to carry [a vessel] through the temple courts. And as he taught them, he said, "Is it not written: 'My house will be called a house of prayer for all nations'? But you have made it 'a den of robbers.'" (Mark 11:15–17)

Most of us are aware of the fact that Jesus shut down the commercial activities in the temple area. Merchants made a profit by selling sacrificial animals there; money changers profited by exchanging Roman coins (with the offensive image of Caesar on them) for temple currency. The merchants and money changers reaped huge profits from this business, and Jesus stormed in and swept the whole mess out.

But He also did something else, something extremely significant though often overlooked. Mark says that Jesus "would not allow anyone to carry [a vessel] through the temple courts." I have inserted the phrase "a vessel" in that statement because that is what the text literally says. The New International Version uses the term *merchandise,* which is not what the original Greek text says. The NIV is a sound translation, but the usage of the word *merchandise* here is not the best choice. Mark is not talking about the merchandise of the traders and money changers at this point. The King James Version accurately states that Jesus would not allow anyone to "carry any vessel through the temple." The word "vessel" refers to a *utensil of worship.* Mark is telling us that Jesus not only shut down the *commerce* of the temple but He also shut down the *religious rituals* of the temple.

Why is this significant? In the Old Testament books of Leviticus and Numbers, God instituted rituals for the temple at Jerusalem. These rituals required the priests to carry many things through the temple area. They had to bring animals into the temple, bind them upon the altar, and slay them. They carried the blood from these sacrifices in basins into the holy place to sprinkle on the altar of incense. Then they had to take the burned carcasses of the sacrifices out again. So there was a continual procession of priests through the temple area all day long, carrying out the system of rituals God Himself had given to the nation of Israel.

But on this day, when Jesus came into the temple He stopped all of the religious rituals in their tracks. He brought to a close—for the first time since the days of the Maccabees in 164 BC—the offerings of Israel. Why? Because Jesus refused to acknowledge the temple worship as having meaning or value any longer. Though the Jewish priests, money changers, and traders went right back to their former activity as soon as Jesus left, and though these practices would continue for forty more years until the Romans destroyed the temple, God no longer accepted those sacrifices.

When Jesus went to the cross as the Lamb of God who takes away the sins of the world, He declared all other sacrifices to be null and void. The Old Testament rituals and sacrifices were mere symbols and shadows pointing to the reality of the true "Lamb of God"—and Jesus Himself was that Reality.

Having stopped the sacrifices, the Lord stood in quiet dignity the next day and pronounced the official sentence of rejection:

> "Look, your house is left to you desolate. For I tell you, you will not see me again until you say, 'Blessed is he who comes in the name of the Lord.'" (Matthew 23:38–39)

Having said this, Jesus left the temple, and the disciples went with Him. Silently, they walked down through the valley of Kidron and up the other side to the Mount of Olives. There Jesus sat down on one of the rocks that overlooked the city and the temple area. The disciples were troubled and confused. They could not understand His actions and words concerning the temple. The temple was the focal point of the nation's life. They regarded it with holy awe as the very dwelling place of God among His people. Its beauty was famous throughout the earth and they could not believe that God would allow any harm to come to it. So they pointed out to Jesus the strength and beauty of the temple. To this, Jesus responded with even more distressing words:

> "Do you see all these things?" he asked. "I tell you the truth, not one stone here will be left on another; every one will be thrown down." (Matthew 24:2)

The disciples were dumbfounded. They could not believe this would ever happen. True, the nation was in bondage under Rome, and the people of Israel had no final authority in their own land. But the Romans had been in power in Palestine for many years and had not harmed the temple. They were lovers of temples, and they generally preserved the temples and monuments in the lands they conquered. There seemed no reason why this temple should ever be destroyed. Yet Jesus solemnly assured His disciples that there would not be one stone of the temple left standing upon another. It would be razed to the ground.

The Test of a Prophet

What was Jesus doing when He predicted the destruction of the temple in Jerusalem? It is easy to miss the significance of His prophecy. The fact is that He is *presenting His credentials as a prophet.* The law of Moses requires that whenever a prophet claims to foretell the future, the prophet must give a sign by which his prophecy can be tested. In Deuteronomy 18, in the midst of a prophecy concerning the coming of the Messiah, Moses said:

> "I will raise up for them a prophet like you from among their brothers; I will put my words in his mouth, and he will tell them everything I command him. If anyone does not listen to my words that the prophet speaks in my name, I myself will call him to account." (Deuteronomy 18:18–19)

Many Bible scholars agree that this prophecy was a foreview of the coming of Jesus Christ. He was that prophet, raised up by God among the people of Israel. He would be like Moses and would speak words that the nation should hear. Moses went on to say:

> "But a prophet who presumes to speak in my name anything I have not commanded him to say, or a prophet who speaks in the name of other gods, must be put to death."
>
> You may say to yourselves, "How can we know when a message has not been spoken by the LORD?" If what a prophet proclaims in the name of the LORD does not take place or come true, that is a message the LORD has not spoken. That

prophet has spoken presumptuously. Do not be afraid of him." (Deuteronomy 18:20–22)

When this admonition was carried out in Israel, it became customary for the prophets to give the people a prediction of something that would occur in the near future. When it came to pass as foretold, the people would know that this was a true and authenticated prophet. But if the sign did not occur as predicted, the prophecy in its entirety was to be rejected as not from God, and the prophet was exposed as false.

So Jesus predicted the downfall of the temple in the near future (about forty years hence) as a sign that all else He included in His discourse was true. This is what lay behind the request of the disciples for a sign associated with His coming.

The parallel account in Luke 21:20 provides additional details of the predicted overthrow of Jerusalem and the temple. In that account Jesus says, "When you see Jerusalem being surrounded by armies, you will know that its desolation is near." Forty years later, the Roman armies commanded by a general named Titus surrounded the city and fulfilled the prediction to the letter. Along with Titus was a Jewish historian named Josephus, who recorded the terrible story in exacting detail. It was one of the most ghastly sieges in the history of warfare. When the Romans came, the city was divided among three warring factions of Jews who fought each other so bitterly that they were unaware of the approaching Roman army until it was too late. The forces of Titus gave the Jews every opportunity to surrender and save their capital from destruction, but the Jewish people refused to give up.

The long siege inflicted a terrible famine on the city. The bodies of the dead citizens of Jerusalem were stacked like cordwood in the streets. Mothers ate their own dead children to preserve themselves.

The toll of Jewish suffering was horrible but they would not surrender.

When the walls were breached at last, Titus tried to preserve the temple by giving orders to his soldiers not to destroy or burn it. But the anger of the soldiers against the Jews was so intense that they disobeyed the order of their general and set fire to the temple. The gold and silver that was stored in the temple melted and ran down between the rocks and into the cracks of the temple stones. The Roman soldiers took long bars and pried the massive stones apart. In the end—just as Jesus had predicted—there was literally not one stone left standing upon another. The temple itself was totally destroyed, though a portion of a wall around the temple area was left partially intact. This lone portion, called the Western Wall, still stands in Jerusalem today.

This prophecy, so remarkably and exactingly fulfilled and confirmed by secular history, is convincing proof that God will fulfill every other part of His plan for the outline of history. As Jesus Himself said when He sat upon the Mount of Olives, "Heaven and earth will pass away, but my words will never pass away" (Matthew 24:35).

Now that we have demonstrated the certainty and reliability of the Lord's Olivet prophecy, let's take a look at the structure of the Olivet discourse as Jesus outlines it for us in these opening verses.

Three Tough Questions

In Matthew 24:3, the disciples ask one question that is actually three questions. They say, "Tell us when will this [the destruction of the temple] happen, and what will be the sign of your coming and of the end of the age?" The three questions embedded in this sentence are:

(1) When will the temple be destroyed?

(2) What will be the sign of your coming?

(3) What will be the sign of the end of the age?

The Lord's answer to the first question, as we have already seen, is recorded in Luke 21:20. The temple would be destroyed after these disciples saw Jerusalem surrounded by armies. A number of these disciples were, in fact, still living when the Roman general Titus fulfilled that prediction.

The second and third questions are perfectly natural in view of the instruction of Moses to demand a sign from those who claim to prophesy in God's name. There is a major difference between what the disciples had in mind when they asked these questions and what we think of when we read them. The disciples asked out of confusion. There were many things they could not see, or would not believe, and so their questions were difficult to answer.

They were like the little boy who asked his father: "Daddy, why does the sun shine in the daytime when we don't need it, and not at night when we do?" That kind of question is difficult to answer not because the answer is so hard but because the question is so wrong.

To a significant degree, we can understand much better than they what their questions meant, for we have the history of twenty centuries to look back upon. We also understand the importance of Christ's death and resurrection—an idea they were not ready to accept. They could not understand all that Jesus said to them. Though He had repeatedly predicted His own death and resurrection, they couldn't conceive of such a thing. Since they would not allow themselves to face the terrible specter of His death, they could not have any clear idea of what He meant when He said He was coming again.

So what did the disciples mean when they asked Him about His coming? They did not picture a second advent. They did not envision Jesus coming from heaven to earth. What they had in mind when they asked about His coming was a *political revolution*, which would lead to Jesus being crowned King and Messiah of Israel.

In this passage, the disciples use an interesting word for "coming." It is the Greek word *parousia*. This word appears four times in Matthew 24—in verses 3, 27, 37, and 39. It is not the usual word for "coming." This word means more than the mere arrival of a person. It also implies that the person will have a *continuing presence* after his arrival. This is important to understand, because the meaning of the entire Olivet discourse turns on the definition of this word *parousia*, or "coming." There are other places in this passage where the English word *coming* is used, but it is not the same Greek word; hence, it conveys a distinctly different meaning.

Even after the Resurrection, the disciples continued to ask Jesus questions that reflected a political concept of His coming. In Acts 1:6 they asked, "Lord, are you at this time going to restore the kingdom to Israel?" They were still expecting Jesus to reign in a political sense over the nations of the earth. He did not deny that this would eventually occur, but He reminded them that the times and seasons are the Father's prerogative to determine.

So when they asked Him on the Mount of Olives, "What will be the sign of your coming?" they were not asking about His return to earth—the Second Coming of Christ. They were asking about His coming into His political and messianic kingship over the nation of Israel.

Like the boy who asked why the sun didn't shine at night when it was needed, these disciples had asked a question that was fundamentally wrong in its assumptions. Yet Jesus treated that question as if it were a legitimate inquiry about His second advent.

The Close of the Age

The disciples also asked for a second sign concerning the close of the age. They do not ask, as the King James Version translates, about "the end of the world." Their question has nothing to do with the end of the world. The world will go on for a long time after the events of the Olivet discourse are fulfilled. What will end is not the world itself but the age in which we live. In this matter they seemed to have a clearer understanding than they did of the Lord's "coming" or *parousia*. Even so, they clearly believed that the "end of the age" lay immediately ahead, not centuries away.

It should not surprise us that the disciples misunderstood the nature of Jesus' message. They had heard Jesus teaching the parables of the kingdom (see Matthew 13) and had heard Him speak of the close of the age when He would send His angels throughout the earth to gather men to judgment. They also knew the Old Testament predictions of how the promised Messiah would reign over the earth. They surely knew of Daniel's remarkable prophecy (see Daniel 9) that there would be a period of 490 years (seventy weeks of years, or 490 years) from the rebuilding of Jerusalem after the Babylonian captivity until the time of Messiah the Prince. From that prophecy, they may well have known that the 490 years were almost completed. Little wonder that they expected the close of the age to be imminent.

What they did not understand and could not be expected to see was that there would be a wide chasm of time between the hour in which they asked their question and the close of the age in the distant future. We cannot blame them for failing to understand this, because it is difficult to distinguish between the two comings of Jesus in the Old Testament prophecies. It is rather like looking at the evening sky and seeing the moon and the planet Venus side by side. They may appear to be side by side, yet the moon is about

240,000 miles away while the planet Venus is at least 25 million miles beyond the moon. Those two objects are literally worlds apart. So it is with the Old Testament prophecies of the Messiah.

Peter wrote that the prophets foresaw "the sufferings of Christ and the glories that would follow" (1 Peter 1:11). But to those ancient prophets, it seemed as if the sufferings and the glories were all part of one great event. What looked to them to be one great mountain range of fulfillment was actually two widely separated ranges with a great valley of time in between.

For instance, Isaiah 9:6 records the well-known prediction of a coming child: "For to us a child is born, to us a son is given." That is a prophecy of our Lord's first advent as a baby in Bethlehem. But the rest of the verse says, "And he will be called Wonderful Counselor, Mighty God, Everlasting Father, Prince of Peace." So the latter part of the verse clearly refers to His reign in the days of a kingdom that will eventually cover the earth. The first half of this verse was fulfilled 2,000 years ago. The second half will not be fulfilled until the Lord returns to earth again. Yet these two events were brought together into a single verse with no hint of any intervening time.

The Sign of the End of the Age

Next, the Lord takes their questions and answers them in reverse order. They asked about the sign of His presence and the sign of the end of the age. He answers the last question first. The sign of the close of the age is found in Matthew 24:15—"So when you see standing in the holy place 'the abomination that causes desolation,' spoken of through the prophet Daniel . . . ." We shall examine that sign later in this book.

Jesus gives the sign of His coming in Matthew 24:30. "At that time the sign of the Son of Man will appear in the sky, and all the nations of the earth will mourn. They will see the Son of Man coming on the clouds of the sky, with power and great glory." This, too, we shall closely examine later in this book. But for now it is important to understand that, throughout the Olivet discourse, Jesus takes pains to make clear to His disciples that the end of the age is an event that takes place in the distant future.

In this great prediction, Jesus illustrates two important principles of prophetic fulfillment: First, God's prophecy is fulfilled according to His timetable, not ours. We cannot know when the fulfillment of a prophecy will take place. Jesus warned in Acts 1:7, "It is not for you to know the times or dates the Father has set by his own authority."

Second, God's prophecy is often subject to what we might call "double fulfillment." In other words, a single prophecy may be fulfilled in two different ways at two different times. For example, Jesus predicted the encirclement and destruction of Jerusalem by hostile armies, and his prophecy was fulfilled just forty years later. But that historic fulfillment was also a preview of another day in the distant future when Jerusalem would again be surrounded by armies and face a time of destruction on a never-before-imagined scale. That second destruction will come at the close of the age in which we now live.

Notice that Jesus spoke to His disciples as though they would live to see all the events He predicted. Obviously, therefore, He was speaking to them as representatives of Israel and of the Christian church. Some of the disciples did in fact live to see the destruction of Jerusalem as Jesus foretold it—but none of them would live to see the end of the age; none would pass through the Great Tribulation.

The disciples were uniquely representative men, because they were both Jewish and Christian. They were men of Israel and men of the church. They represented the nation of Israel and God's dealings with that remarkable people. But after the cross and Pentecost they were Christians, part of the church, so they also belonged to the unique body, the Christian church, that would fulfill God's purpose throughout the intervening centuries before the end times. So the message Jesus spoke on Mount Olivet includes truth for the church in its relationship to the present age, and also truth for Israel in its time of trouble at the end of the age.

As Jesus sat on that mountainside, facing the darkest hour of His life, He knew about the scheming of His enemies, the betrayal that Judas planned, the frailty and unreliability of His friends, and more. The very disciples who clustered around Him, to whom He entrusted this message, would forsake and deny Him within a few short hours. He saw the darkness of those next few hours, but He looked beyond those moments of suffering to the light and glory that lay beyond. Though everything around Him seemed utterly hopeless, He quietly and resolutely declared what the end would be, without a hint of uncertainty or doubt.

All things, He said, find their significance and meaning in relationship to Him. Any event not related to His purpose in the age is without meaning or significance. As we listen to His declaration of the outline of human history, we face the inevitable question: How does my life relate to these great events? Am I contributing to the anarchy and horror of the last days, or am I part of the eternal program of God, a program that is bringing human history to its appointed climax? When the Son of God returns to establish His kingdom on the earth, will I rejoice to see Him? Or will I despair, knowing that I am about to be judged for my sin and rebellion against Him?

We do not live our lives in an isolated segment of time. All the events of human history are interwoven into a great plan that is bringing the Olivet prophecy to pass. We are either working in concert with God's eternal plan—or we will be swept away by it. What part are you playing in the great events that Jesus prophesied from the Olivet mountainside?

These are the questions that confront us in the Olivet discourse. These are the questions that, as we move through the coming pages, you must answer for yourself. ◇

2

The Age of Deception

Matthew 24:4–14

In 1925, followers of the Indian mystic Krishnamurti built a 200-seat amphitheater overlooking the harbor of Sydney, Australia. From this amphitheater, members of Krishnamurti's Order of the Star of the East planned to await the Second Coming of Christ. Krishnamurti had promised that Jesus would walk across the waters of the Pacific Ocean and greet the followers of the Indian mystic in the amphitheater. Several years passed, and Jesus didn't return. In 1929, the group of followers dissolved, and Krishnamurti went on to other religious pursuits. Where the amphitheater once stood, there is a block of apartment buildings today.

The history of religion is filled with such stories. Again and again, various groups, cults, and congregations have decided upon a date for the Lord's return. Then they have sold everything they had and gone to a beach or a hilltop or a rooftop to await the Second Coming—only to be bitterly disappointed.

Jesus knew that there would be many religious leaders claiming to speak for Him while leading their followers astray. That is why Jesus, in Matthew 24:4, emphatically says, "Watch out that no one deceives you."

At every stage of the Christian era, there has been much confusion over the time of the Lord's return. This confusion continues in our own age. But you and I don't have to be confused by the times or deceived by false, misguided, or self-serving religious leaders. Jesus has given us the truth of His coming in the Olivet discourse. No, He didn't pinpoint the day and the hour—but He did give us all the information we will ever need to live wisely and faithfully as we await His return.

Don't Be Deceived!

If there is one word that dominates the Olivet discourse, it is the word "deception" in its various forms. The age Jesus describes in the Olivet prophecy is a time of great confusion and deception. There will be widespread uncertainty about the meaning of the events of this age, and people will be easily misled. So Jesus warns in verse 4, "Watch out that no one deceives you."

He amplifies this warning in verse 5, where He adds, "For many will come in my name, claiming, 'I am the Christ,' and will deceive many." Again in verse 11 He says: "And many false prophets will appear and deceive many people." And once again in verse 24: "For false Christs and false prophets will appear and perform great signs and miracles to deceive even the elect—if that were possible."

Again and again, Jesus warns against being deceived—and He tells us how to avoid being deceived: "Watch out!" In other words, Keep your eyes open! Don't be gullible—test those who claim to speak for God! Demonstrate godly skepticism to keep from being confused and deceived.

Then Jesus proceeded to show the disciples that they were already confused in thinking that the end of the age lay immediately ahead of them. From verse 5 through verse 14, Jesus plainly showed that there will be a long (though indeterminate) period of time before the end of the age. These disciples knew from the prophet Daniel that the end of the age would not be a single spectacular event, but rather a series of events covering several years. So the Lord carefully traced the age which they could not see—an age that is the very parenthesis of time in which we now live.

Jesus chooses His words carefully in the Olivet discourse, and we should heed them carefully. Many people get the wrong impression of Jesus' meaning. They read, for example, verse 6, in which Jesus says, "You will hear of wars and rumors of wars, but see to it that you are not alarmed. Such things must happen, but the end is still to come." I've heard many Bible commentators and pastors say that "wars and rumors of wars" are "signs of the times," signs that the end is near. But that is not what Jesus says. In fact, He says the very opposite! Jesus says clearly that if you hear of wars and rumors of wars, don't be alarmed because these events *do not* signal the end! Such events, He says in verse 8, are merely "the beginning of birth pains." So Jesus does not give us the "signs of the times" here.

In verses 9 to 14, He lists a number of evil events that will come: Believers will be persecuted, hated, and killed for the sake of Christ; some will turn away from the faith and betray true believers; false prophets will appear, deceiving many; wickedness will increase and love will grow cold. Jesus is saying, in effect, "These events all lead up to the end of the age, but they are not signs that the end has arrived."

What, then, are the *true* signs of the end of the age? He gives the first such sign in verse 14: "And this gospel of the kingdom will be preached in the whole world as a testimony to all nations, and then the end will come." Then, in verses 15 through 31, Jesus gives a detailed account of the events of the end of the age.

Because we live in this time before the end of the age, this time of growing confusion and deception, it is important for us to understand the events Jesus outlines in His prophecy. As we have seen, the dominant theme of the Olivet discourse is "Don't be deceived!" Jesus warns us against the allure of the false, the glamour of the phony. Deception is the pervasive threat that drenches human minds, turning people away from the unseen spiritual kingdom and toward a reliance upon what can be seen and touched in the material world.

Deception is at the heart of a series of perils that Jesus warns us about in the Olivet discourse. Once each of these perils is introduced into human society, it will continue to rule over human minds until the end of the age. Those perils are: (1) false messiahs; (2) wars and rumors of wars; (3) natural calamity; (4) persecution; (5) apostasy; and (6) cynicism. Let's take a focused look at each of these perils, all of which are a part of our world.

Peril 1: False Messiahs

Matthew 24:5 introduces us to the peril of false messiahs, of counterfeit Christs. Jesus says, "For many will come in my name, claiming, 'I am the Christ,' and will deceive many."

The apostle John wrote at the close of the first century, "Even now many antichrists have come. . . . They went out from us, but they did not really belong to us" (1 John 2:18–19). The term *antichrist* does not indicate someone who is openly against Christ, such as an atheist or a pagan. Rather it is a person who subtly undermines true Christianity by substituting a false and deceptive "Christianity." An antichrist is a counterfeit Christ, a false messiah. ("Christ" is the Greek form of the Hebrew word "Messiah.")

Who, then, are the false christs that Jesus warns us against? Certainly this would include the originators and propagators of all the false cults that have arisen throughout the course of this age, from the first century to the twenty-first. We have witnessed the rise of many cults in the past few decades—groups that have a Christian flavor and may even speak highly of Christ but which alter and twist His message. They downgrade His deity, diminish the value of His sacrifice on the cross, or substitute subtle deception in the place of the simple truths of biblical Christianity. Some of the more obvious of these cults are the Jehovah's Witnesses, Mormonism, Christian Science, and the Church of Scientology. But the spirit of antichrist has also reared its deceptive head in many mainstream Protestant denominations.

Some denominations are now debating whether the claim of Jesus in John 14:6 is still valid: "I am the way and the truth and the life. No one comes to the Father except through me." A few of these denominations have concluded that Jesus is merely *one* way, not *the* way; there are many paths to God, they say. These denominations have been led into error and deception by the spirit of antichrist.

So it is a mistake to think that antichrists are found only in such obvious places as the pseudochristian cults. They are sometimes found in the highest levels of our oldest and most prestigious Christian denominations. It is exactly as Peter predicted when he wrote that "there will be false teachers among you. They will secretly introduce destructive heresies, even denying the sovereign Lord who bought them—bringing swift destruction on themselves" (2 Peter 2:1).

Individuals, groups, and churches that seem outwardly Christian in their talk and behavior, yet reject the true Jesus Christ of the Bible, are antichrists—counterfeit christs, false messiahs. Any person or organization that purports to be Christian but does not present the biblically complete and accurate picture of Christ is antichrist. It is the rise of such groups that our Lord predicts. The subtle deception spread by these groups and individuals, both within and outside the true Christian church, poses a tremendous danger to faith.

So cults are a deceptive danger to faith, and so are churches that have been invaded and infected by the spirit of antichrist. But there are other antichristian voices that surround us, threatening to undermine and destroy our faith through deceptive means. Some false messiahs come with a bold proclamation, such as "I am the Messiah" or "Our group has the true Christian message." But other false messiahs are more subtle. They do not openly confront the Christian faith, but instead they seek to lure us away from it.

Some antichrists may come to us as political or patriotic movements, like the messianic political movement the disciples thought Jesus had in mind when He preached about a coming kingdom. Many people today believe that the salvation of society and of the individual lies in some political "ism"—liberalism, conservatism, libertarianism, socialism, and so forth. While patriotism and conscientious political involvement are good things, they are not a substitute for Christ and His salvation.

Some antichrists may come to us as social movements, charitable organizations, and activism on behalf of various causes from the environment to human rights to feeding the hungry. Meeting human need and caring for the Earth are Christian obligations commended to us in the Scriptures, but social and charitable action are not the same thing as faith in Christ. In fact, some people—including many who claim to be Christians—have substituted social action in place of Jesus, offering to lead people into "peace" with God through caring activities, a "peace" without the cross and without forgiveness of sin. This is a false peace, based on deception. If we allow good things like social activism to replace an authentic saving relationship with Christ, then those things are an antichrist in our lives, destroying true faith—and we have allowed ourselves to be deceived.

Peril 2: Wars and Rumors of Wars

The second peril Jesus foresees is that of conflict—of "wars and rumors of wars." He says:

> "You will hear of wars and rumors of wars, but see to it
> that you are not alarmed. Such things must happen, but the
> end is still to come. Nation will rise against nation, and king-
> dom against kingdom." (Matthew 24:6–7)

Clearly, Jesus is not predicting any one specific war or revolution. He is characterizing the general course of the age. It will be marked by continual turmoil among nations, producing a torrent of fear, death, horror, terror, and misery. His words telescope together all the effects that war can produce in the human heart.

War is a powerful threat to faith. Many a young man has been deceived by the "glory" of war and has left home to proudly march against the enemy. But amid the carnage and butchery and sheer, stark terror of battle, his eyes have been opened. If he survives at all, he returns home disillusioned, sickened, and embittered by all he has witnessed and experienced.

War is often used by atheists and agnostics as a reason for rejecting faith in God. One writer for *The American Atheist* commented on a tribal war in Africa in which a half a million people died, most of them hacked and butchered by machetes. At least 100,000 of the victims were children. "If there is a god," this atheist observed, "he is intensely cruel. . . . By what great irrationality can we possibly believe that there is a god who, having completely neglected those precious, mutilated children, nevertheless has concern for us?"

This is a deceptive question, for it ignores the obvious fact of human free will. It is impossible for human beings to have free will unless they are free to do evil. God did not cause this slaughter, nor did He cause the Holocaust or any other war or genocide in history. True, He didn't stop it—but the only way He could stop it is to overrule human free will, and that He will not do. When we human beings choose to terrorize each other and slaughter one another, He can do nothing but weep with us and agonize with us. But He will not take away from us the terrible, awesome gift of free will.

Men who choose not to believe in God will continue to use human evil as an excuse for their unbelief. But war is something we do to each other, not something God has done to us.

Peril 3: Natural Calamity

Another peril to faith that Jesus foresees is the peril of natural calamities. He says:

> "There will be famines and earthquakes in various places.
> All these are the beginning of birth pains." (Matthew 24:7–8)

Natural catastrophes have occurred for as long as history has been recorded. Famines are described in Genesis, Ruth, and elsewhere in the Old Testament. And earthquakes are mentioned in 1 Kings, Amos, and other Old Testament books. Natural calamities have always been a part of human existence. They are not "signs of the times." In the Olivet discourse, Jesus states that during the intervening age in which we live, there will be famines, pestilence, earthquakes, and other natural disasters. Whenever such events occur, they are a threat to faith in God.

Christians sometimes try to convince skeptics that God is love by parading the evidence of nature. They describe the beauty of the sunset, the glory of the mountains, the abundant provision in the natural world for the needs of man. But what becomes of that argument when tornadoes and earthquakes destroy homes and schools, burying children in the ruins? What becomes of that argument when famine destroys life and hope, leaving thousands of children with distended, malnourished bodies? Where, then, is the argument for the love of God as revealed in nature?

How do you preach God's love to those who are fleeing the horrible wrath of a volcano or the thundering destruction of a hurricane? Who has not doubted the Christian faith in the face of such natural calamities as a devastating plague or a ship-swallowing typhoon. It is one thing to say that God is not responsible for war, which is attributable to human free will—but how do we square the reality of natural calamities with our belief in a God who rules and reigns in the midst of all human and natural events?

Granted, our doubts can be answered by a clearer understanding of the purposes and workings of God. But many people who suffer pain, grief, and loss due to a natural calamity are led to a conclusion that an all-loving, all-powerful God could not possibly allow such calamities to happen. I have known people whose faith was scorched and even burned completely away by the fires of natural calamity.

When terrible things happen to good people, we must watch out, as Jesus warns, that we are not deceived or led astray. We must learn the art of clinging tightly in the darkness to what we have learned in the light.

Peril 4: Persecution

Another terrible threat to faith is the threat of persecution. Jesus describes this peril in these words:

> "Then you will be handed over to be persecuted and put to death, and you will be hated by all nations because of me." (Matthew 24:9)

The peril of religious persecution has been an aspect of the Christian life since the very beginning. The persecution of Christians began shortly after the day of Pentecost, when Stephen and James were slain and the disciples scattered. In the ensuing twenty centuries, Christians have been thrown to lions, burned as human torches, mangled by wild beasts, killed by gladiators, drawn apart by horses, and martyred in numerous other dreadful ways.

When we hear about such oppression, we tend to think of the first few centuries of the Christian era, or the persecution that broke out at the time of the Reformation. Many of these crimes are laid out in gruesome detail in *Foxe's Book of Martyrs*.

But the greatest time of persecution of Christians was not the first century or the sixteenth. It was the twentieth century! More Christians have died for their faith in our own time than in any other century in history. More Christians were tortured and slain in one twelve-month period during World War II than died under Rome in all the early centuries. Some authorities estimate the death toll of Christians under communism (including the Soviet Union, the Eastern bloc in Europe, China, and other Asian communist nations) at over 15 million souls! Since Christianity began, no generation has seen such worldwide persecution as has been taking place in our own lifetime.

Living in freedom and prosperity in America, we can scarcely imagine the cost of discipleship in certain parts of the world. In many Islamic nations, for example, Muslims who convert to Christianity are often subject to execution by the state—if the convert's own family doesn't kill him first! Other believers are tortured or enslaved for their faith.

Ask yourself: Would you want to be a Christian if it could cost you your freedom, your livelihood, your comfort, or your very life? How attractive would the gospel of Jesus Christ seem if you could be tortured and killed for receiving it? Jesus spoke of seed that would fall on shallow ground and spring up, but when the sun came out in burning heat, it would wither and die. How many Christians would there be in America if persecution suddenly broke out across the land? Many of us can be cowed into an embarrassed silence at just the hint of being laughed at for our faith. If our faith is so weak that it cannot stand up under a little ridicule, how could we hold on to our faith if the cost of discipleship included being burned at the stake?

Persecution is a cruel and relentless enemy of faith.

Peril 5: Apostasy

Next, the Lord identified another ever-present danger to faith—the peril of apostasy. He said:

> "At that time many will turn away from the faith and will betray and hate each other, and many false prophets will appear and deceive many people. Because of the increase of wickedness, the love of most will grow cold." (Matthew 24:10–12)

Now it becomes clear that we are seeing signs of the approaching end of the age. The symptoms Jesus has listed for us demonstrate a gradually increasing manifestation of evil. We see in these words of Jesus the very same thing we see on our TV screens and read about in our newspaper headlines. Standards that were once respected and upheld are now sneered at and held in contempt.

"At that time many will turn away from the faith and will betray and hate each other," Jesus says. He describes here the terrible pressure of apostasy. When combined with persecution it produces a powerful double attack upon a faith in Christ. It is hard to stand alone against the pressure of apostasy. When we see that everyone has forsaken the faith, when we feel that others have betrayed us and turned away from us, then it becomes easier to succumb to the pressure, to surrender to the attack.

The apostle Paul knew the pain of this kind of pressure. He had a close friend named Demas whom he mentioned fondly in Colossians 4:14 and Philemon 1:24. But near the end of his life, writing from a prison in Rome, he told his friend Timothy, "Demas, because he loved this world, has deserted me and has gone to Thessalonica" (2 Timothy 4:10). Paul's grief and sense of betrayal are poignant and palpable. He had suffered a shattering emotional blow from a trusted fellow worker and friend—a friend who had surrendered to apostasy.

The pressure of apostasy is as severe now as it ever was. This world offers many seductive pleasures and many antichristian pressures. It is harder than ever before to maintain standards of moral and sexual purity. The belief in moral relativism is rampant in our society. Few remain who believe in absolute standards or absolute truth. The church is rapidly accommodating itself to the world rather than setting the standard for holiness and godliness.

So it is not surprising that the faith of many today is trembling and even reeling under relentless hammer-blows of apostasy.

Peril 6: Cynicism

Look again at these words of Jesus: ". . . many false prophets will appear and deceive many people. Because of the increase of wickedness, the love of most will grow cold" (Matthew 24:10–12). Here, Jesus warns of the peril of cynicism—that cold and unfeeling indifference that arises out of increasing wickedness and the teaching of false prophets and counterfeit Christs.

Who are these "false prophets" Jesus warns against? They are not necessarily religious people. Jesus previously warned of false messiahs, of people who would come claiming, "I am the Christ." False messiahs would unquestionably be religious people, but when Jesus talks about "false prophets" I am convinced that He has a much broader definition in mind. By "prophet" He is referring to anyone who claims to speak authoritatively—philosophers, professors, scientists, and statesmen, as well as false clergy and cult gurus. A false prophet is anyone who is a leader of people and whose teachings help to shape our society and influence the thinking of the common man.

What do these secular false prophets teach? They may teach the sanctity of the self, the religion of me-ism, the dogma of insisting on "my rights." The true prophet insists on the rights of God, but the false prophet serves the deceptive message of Satan, with which that serpent first deceived Adam and Eve: "ye shall be as gods" (Genesis 3:5, KJV). In other words, elevate the self, seek your own interests above all, look out for Number One! We see this kind of selfish cynicism pervading our society, producing an avalanche of wickedness, lawlessness, and lovelessness throughout our society.

The overthrow of moral boundaries always destroys love. Those who feel they can live without moral boundaries invariably grow hard, callous, and cynical. They become people who know the price of everything and the value of nothing. Their lives become an endless quest for new pleasures, new experiences, because that is the drug they use to numb the pain of their meaningless, empty existence.

In the headlines all around us we see the evidence of love growing cold: Mothers who murder their own children; cruel, perverted men who prey on children; child pornography; and many more acts of unimaginable sins against the most innocent and helpless among us. "Jesus loves the little children," says the beloved Sunday school song. But in our society we increasingly find that the love of many has grown cold toward these little children Jesus loves.

He Who Endures

These six perils form a list of antichristian currents that flow throughout our society today: (1) false messiahs; (2) wars and rumors of wars; (3) natural calamity; (4) persecution; (5) apostasy; and (6) cynicism. These powerful currents combine to form a vast, nearly irresistible tide of deception, flooding human minds with delusion, sweeping human lives over the brink of destruction and into the raging waters of the world's last day.

These six perils, Jesus says, are the clanging gongs that will sound loudly throughout this age, attempting to drown out that still small voice of faith. How can anyone resist these perils to faith? Who is equal to these intense pressures? Who has the wisdom to distinguish the truth from error amid the thundering din of these clanging gongs of deception?

Fortunately, Jesus does not leave us with this bleak picture. He goes on to a further unveiling of truth. He reveals the secret of power—the power to stand against deception and delusion. He introduces the secret with a small but all-important word: *but*. Jesus says:

> "But he who stands firm to the end will be saved. And this gospel of the kingdom will be preached in the whole world as a testimony to all nations, and then the end will come." (Matthew 24:13–14)

The warning of Jesus is that there will be pressures, there will be deception, there will be both swift, rushing currents of antichristian culture and subtle lures of temptation that will call human souls toward destruction. But the reassurance of Jesus is that those who refuse to be deceived, who stand firm upon the truth, will be saved. Some will endure to the end. They will not be overthrown. They will be saved.

The end referred to here is not the end of the age. After all, it would be humanly impossible for anyone to live through the entire twenty centuries (or more) of this intervening age. What Jesus means here is the end of life.

These words of Jesus have sometimes been distorted to suggest that if someone does his best to hang on and live a good clean life, then he will be saved. But that interpretation takes the Lord's true meaning and turns it completely around. What He actually means is this: If a person is truly saved, then that person will endure to the end. The fact that he endures is proof that he is saved.

In any race a good beginning is meaningless without a strong finish. But it is equally true that a strong finish accomplishes little without a good beginning. Only those who have genuinely found Christ will endure to the end. We cannot stand firm in the faith without an unceasing flow of power. Why? Because, as Jesus has told us, believers are exposed to a relentless flow of pressure! We need to continually renew our strength for the battle against the unceasing forces arrayed against us. We can stand firm against these forces only if we are plugged into the continuous current of God's power.

The reality of God's presence in the lives of authentic believers is revealed not only in the fact that they *stand* in God's power but also in the fact that they *speak* in God's power. When believers speak, the gospel of the kingdom goes forth. Jesus says:

> "And this gospel of the kingdom will be preached in the whole world as a testimony to all nations, and then the end will come." (Matthew 24:14)

The gospel of the kingdom reveals the secret of their ability to stand. Everywhere they go, they tell the story of the One who "has rescued us from the dominion of darkness and brought us into the kingdom of the Son he loves" (Colossians 1:13). Amid the pressures of the age, they reveal that they have heard and obeyed the good news. They stand—but they do not stand alone. The One who stands with them has imparted His life to them. He keeps them safe against the deception of this fallen and dying world.

The Lord Himself said, "My sheep listen to my voice; I know them, and they follow me" (John 10:27). Let the wolves howl, let the bears growl, let the wind moan through the trees—the Lord's sheep will not stray because they know the Shepherd's voice and they will follow Him, no matter what.

Why? Because, as Jesus goes on to say, "I give them eternal life, and they shall never perish; no one can snatch them out of my hand. My Father, who has given them to me, is greater than all; no one can snatch them out of my Father's hand" (John 10:28–29). This is the promise that enables His followers to stand amid the flood of deception and persecution that washes the rest of the world to destruction. His followers will move against the antichristian flood, sometimes bleeding, sometimes in tears, sometimes under a crushing load of pain and loneliness—but never defeated, never surrendering. His authentic followers will never yield. Those who are saved stand firm.

No One Knows the Hour

When the good news of the kingdom has been preached as a testimony to all nations, then shall the end of the age begin, says Jesus. That is one unmistakable mark of the approaching end. It is supremely significant that this present generation is the first generation in twenty long centuries of which it can be truly said: In this generation, the gospel has been preached to all nations. This is properly a "sign of the times" which marks the near approach of the end.

When the alarms and sirens of the Last Day begin to clang and wail, when the people of this world rush in panic and terror, looking for some way of escape, then the deceitfulness of this age will be fully unveiled. Only those who have learned to walk in His truth, day by day, will be empowered by God to endure to the end.

As the deceptive character of this age is revealed, the terrible importance of Jesus' exhortation will also be revealed: "Therefore keep watch, because you do not know on what day your Lord will come" (Matthew 24:42). Are you watching? Are you ready for the Lord's return? Have you received into yourself the life of the One who says, "I am the way and the truth, and the life"?

Has He come to indwell you, to strengthen and keep you every day by a continuous infusion of His life-giving power? Without His life in you, there is no way you can stand against this age of deception.

But if His life is in you, there is no way you can fall. You will stand—that is His promise to you. The test of the reality of your faith is your endurance. If you endure and stand firm to the end of life, then you will have shown that you are saved. Only those who stand have truly known Him; only those who truly know Him will stand. ◇

3

The Worship of Man

———

If you are old enough, you likely remember the furor that arose in 1966 when Beatle John Lennon announced, "Christianity will go. It will vanish and shrink. . . . We're more popular than Jesus now."

But few people know what was going on inside John Lennon's mind at the time he made that statement. In his book *The Quarrymen*, British journalist and Beatle biographer Hunter Davies describes a strange incident that took place about the same time Lennon made his "more popular than Jesus" statement. John Lennon and a longtime friend, Pete Shotton, had been sitting in an apartment taking drugs and listening to music. "Pete," Lennon said, "I think I'm Jesus Christ."

"You what?" asked Shotton. He thought the Beatle was joking.

"I'm Jesus Christ," said Lennon, completely serious. "I'm back again. I've got to tell the world who I am."

The next morning, Lennon had Shotton call an emergency meeting of the board of Apple Records, the recording company founded by the Beatles. The other three Beatles—Paul McCartney, George Harrison, and Ringo Starr—showed up, along with various members of the Apple organization. They found Lennon sitting behind his desk.

"I've something important to tell you all," Lennon said. "I am Jesus Christ. I have come back again."

Everyone was stunned. No one said a word in reply. Finally, someone suggested that they go to lunch.

In the restaurant, the Beatles and Apple people were sitting together at a table and a man came into the restaurant and recognized them. He came over to Lennon and said, "How nice to meet you, Mr. Lennon. How are you?"

"I'm Jesus Christ," Lennon said.

"Oh, really?" the man said. "Well, I really liked your last record."

John Lennon is neither the first nor the last in a long line of people who have falsely claimed to be Jesus. The Bible warns us that we must "test the spirits" so that we can sort out God's truth from the "spirit of the antichrist, which you have heard is coming and even now is already in the world" (1 John 4:3). Jesus has already warned of the many false Christs and false prophets who would appear in the days before the end of the age.

Now, as we come to a key passage, Matthew 24:15–22, Jesus tightens the focus of His prophecy, from many antichrists to a single Antichrist—the man of lawlessness who was predicted in strikingly similar terms by the prophet Daniel, the apostle Paul, the apostle John, and the Lord Jesus Christ.

Let the Reader Understand . . .

"And then the end will come."

With those dramatic words, the Olivet prophecy of Jesus zooms in on that specific point in time called "the end of the age." Up till now, Jesus has given us a telescopic view of at least twenty centuries between Jesus' first and second advents—a time of mounting pressure and deception. Now Jesus focuses on the all-important sign of the close of the age. He says:

> "So when you see standing in the holy place 'the abomination that causes desolation,' spoken of through the prophet Daniel—let the reader understand—then let those who are in Judea flee to the mountains. Let no one on the roof of his house go down to take anything out of the house. Let no one in the field go back to get his cloak. How dreadful it will be in those days for pregnant women and nursing mothers! Pray that your flight will not take place in winter or on the Sabbath. For then there will be great distress, unequaled from the beginning of the world until now—and never to be equaled again. If those days had not been cut short, no one would survive, but for the sake of the elect those days will be shortened." (Matthew 24:15–22)

The Lord's language here is the most somber He could employ. He speaks of a time of trouble that is coming, the like of which has never been seen in human history. It will be a time of unprecedented death, destruction, suffering, and terror. There have been many catastrophic moments in history, but never like this one. For those who will be living in Judea, the region in and around Jerusalem, it will be a time to act promptly and flee the city.

These words are so intensely important that we must not hurry over them. In fact, the apostle Matthew underscores their importance with the phrase "let the reader understand." He is warning us that there are truths embedded in these words of our Lord that are not apparent on the surface. We need to ponder and understand all the crucial meaning to be found here. Most important of all, we must compare this passage to other Scripture passages, especially the book of Daniel, which Jesus specifically mentions.

Daniel's Prophecy

First, let's examine the sign Jesus gives us that signals the close of the age. It will be, He says, "'the abomination that causes desolation,' spoken of through the prophet Daniel." It is significant that Jesus cites the book of Daniel.

No book of the Old Testament has been as mistreated and scorned by critics as the prophecy of Daniel. Liberal commentators have questioned its authorship, claiming it was written not by the prophet Daniel but by an unknown writer who lived no more than a 100 to 160 years before Christ. The prophetic content of the book has been denied and ridiculed. In many ways, it has been more viciously attacked than any other book in the Bible.

The liberal critics of Daniel have a strong motivation for attacking this prophecy. By discounting the authenticity of the book of Daniel, they hope to undermine all biblical prophecy, as well as the validity of the Bible and the authority of Jesus. Since Jesus quotes from Daniel, they reason, then He must either be ignorant or a liar, since the book of Daniel (according to them) is a fraud and not a true prophecy. The book of Daniel is also the Old Testament source of the phrase "Son of Man" as a designation for the Messiah—a term that Jesus often used in referring to Himself. If the critics can undermine the reputation of Daniel's prophecy, then they have struck a blow against the Lord's claim to be the promised Messiah.

But the critics of Daniel have a number of problems. For example, if Daniel was written around 100 BC, then the book of Ezekiel, which cites the prophecy of Daniel, must also have a late and spurious origin. Yet there is very good evidence that Ezekiel is much older than that. Also, recent archaeological discoveries confirm the accuracy of Daniel as history. For example, the discovery of an inscribed clay tablet called "the Chronicle of Nabonidus" confirms Daniel's historical validity and dashes critics' claims that the kings named in Daniel's prophecy never existed. The Dead Sea Scrolls contain eight copies of Daniel, more than any other manuscript, which affirms the high esteem that was accorded Daniel's prophecy by the strict Essenes who hid the scrolls.

Moreover, it is sheer arrogance for any person who calls himself a Christian (as many liberal critics do) to take a view of Scripture that contradicts the views of Christ Himself. Jesus regarded the book of Daniel as a valid and true prophecy, inspired by the Holy Spirit, and accurate in every detail. If the prophecy of Daniel is not valid, then the history of Daniel is a lie, and Jesus, who validated the book of Daniel, is either deceived or a liar Himself. But, of course, Jesus is neither deceived nor a deceiver. The word of our Lord is true, and so is the prophetic word God spoke to us through His servant, Daniel.

The sign our Lord refers to—"the abomination that causes desolation"—is mentioned in Daniel at least three times. It is the sign of a man who offers himself to the Jews to be worshiped as God. The disciples clearly understood that Jesus was referring to Daniel's prediction of the coming of a man who would take away the continual burnt offering of the Jews. In place of the burnt offerings, this man would present himself as "the abomination that causes desolation" or the desolating sacrilege. Here is how Daniel describes that man:

> "In the latter part of their reign [that is, the rule of certain kings who will come upon the scene in the Middle East], when rebels have become completely wicked [the time when evil has come to its full expression], a stern-faced king, a master of intrigue, will arise. He will become very strong, but not by his own power. He will cause astounding devastation and will succeed in whatever he does. He will destroy the mighty

men and the holy people. He will cause deceit to prosper, and he will consider himself superior. When they feel secure, he will destroy many and take his stand against the Prince of princes. Yet he will be destroyed, but not by human power.

"The vision of the evenings and mornings that has been given you is true, but seal up the vision, for it concerns the distant future." (Daniel 8:23–26)

A Double Fulfillment

Note that Daniel was told that the vision "concerns the distant future." Liberal critics insist that this vision was fulfilled in the turbulent days of the Maccabees in 168–165 BC, when a Syrian king, Antiochus Epiphanes, desecrated the temple in Jerusalem. Antiochus offered a sow upon the altar, then erected a statue of Jupiter (called *Zeus* by the Greeks) to be worshiped. The desecration committed by Antiochus was undoubtedly a preview of the future and the final "abomination that causes desolation." But the desecration by Antiochus could not have been the fulfillment of Daniel's prophecy, or Jesus would not have said, some 165 years after Antiochus, that men could yet expect to see "'the abomination that causes desolation,' spoken of through the prophet Daniel" standing in the holy place.

Another reference to this sacrilege is found in Daniel 9. This reference is found in the midst of an amazing prophecy known as the Vision of the Seventy Weeks—amazing because it is so specific and precise, and has already proven to be astoundingly accurate. The Vision of the Seventy Weeks was an announcement to Daniel by the angel Gabriel that God had marked off a period of 490 years (seventy weeks of years), which would begin when the Persian king,

Artaxerxes, issued a command to rebuild the walls of Jerusalem. Artaxerxes made his proclamation in 445 BC. The 490-year period would terminate with a time of terrible trouble during which a coming prince would cause the Jewish sacrifices to cease and would thus establish the "the abomination that causes desolation."

The angel Gabriel told Daniel that, after the command of Artaxerxes was issued, a period of first seven, and then sixty-two, of those seven-year "weeks" (a total of 483 years) would end just before the Messiah would be "cut off." In counting 483 years from 445 BC to the date of the crucifixion of Christ, allowance must be made for a four-year error in the date of Christ's birth; Jesus would have actually been born in 4 BC on the Gregorian calendar, not AD 1. Allowance must also be made for the fact that the ancient Hebrews used a 360-day calendar. A period of indeterminate length would then intervene before the seventieth or final "week" (seven years). During that unfixed period of time, the city of Jerusalem would be destroyed and the Jews would endure wars and desolations until the end. Here are the angel Gabriel's actual words to Daniel:

> "After the sixty-two 'sevens,' the Anointed One [that is, Messiah] will be cut off and will have nothing [a clear reference to the crucifixion]. The people of the ruler who will come will destroy the city and the sanctuary [this was fulfilled under the Roman general Titus forty years after the crucifixion]. The end will come like a flood: War will continue until the end, and desolations have been decreed. He [the prince who is to come] will confirm a covenant with many for one 'seven.' In the middle of the 'seven' he will put an end to sacrifice and offering. And on a wing of the temple he will set up an abomination that causes desolation, until the end that is decreed is poured out on him." (Daniel 9:26–27)

There is one more glimpse of this "prince who is to come" in Daniel 11:36–39. There he is called simply "the king." Daniel records:

> "The king will do as he pleases. He will exalt and magnify himself above every god and will say unheard-of things against the God of gods. He will be successful until the time of wrath is completed, for what has been determined must take place. He will show no regard for the gods of his fathers or for the one desired by women, nor will he regard any god, but will exalt himself above them all. Instead of them, he will honor a god of fortresses; a god unknown to his fathers he will honor with gold and silver, with precious stones and costly gifts. He will attack the mightiest fortresses with the help of a foreign god and will greatly honor those who acknowledge him. He will make them rulers over many people and will distribute the land at a price." (Daniel 11:36–39)

All of these passages in Daniel agree concerning the coming of a man who shall fulfill our Lord's prediction. The appearance of that man on the world scene is the sign of the end of the age. There are other references in Scripture to this man. Paul describes his coming in his second letter to the Thessalonians:

> Don't let anyone deceive you in any way, for that day will not come until the rebellion occurs and the man of lawlessness is revealed, the man doomed to destruction. He will oppose and will exalt himself over everything that is called God or is worshiped, so that he sets himself up in God's temple, proclaiming himself to be God. (2 Thessalonians 2:3–4)

And we find another unmistakable description of this man in the book of Revelation. The apostle John writes:

The beast was given a mouth to utter proud words and blasphemies and to exercise his authority for forty-two months. He opened his mouth to blaspheme God, and to slander his name and his dwelling place and those who live in heaven. He was given power to make war against the saints and to conquer them. And he was given authority over every tribe, people, language and nation. All inhabitants of the earth will worship the beast—all whose names have not been written in the book of life belonging to the Lamb that was slain from the creation of the world. (Revelation 13:5–8)

Before He spoke this prophecy on the Mount of Olives, Jesus made a fascinating prophecy to the religious leaders who opposed him. He said, "I have come in my Father's name, and you do not accept me; but if someone else comes in his own name, you will accept him" (John 5:43). If you did not read those words carefully, you might miss the fact that this, too, is a prophecy about the man of lawlessness—the coming Antichrist. The statement is oblique—yet it is unmistakable: Jesus is addressing the religious leaders as representatives of those who, centuries hence, will worship the man who comes in his own name, demanding that all the inhabitants of the earth worship him.

The coming Antichrist will symbolize and personify all that stands against God. There are many other references to him in the Old Testament prophets, and we do not have the space to consider them all. But briefly, I believe that the first prophecy of the Antichrist may well occur in Genesis 3:15. God tells the serpent of Eden, "And I will put enmity between you and the woman, and between your offspring [a possible reference to the Antichrist, the "offspring" of Satan] and hers [Jesus, the offspring of the woman]; he [Jesus] will crush your head, and you will strike his heel [a reference to the Crucifixion—Jesus is wounded by death but rises again, a costly victory that crushes the head of Satan]." For other Old Testament passages that likely refer to the Antichrist, see Psalm 74:8–10; Psalm 110:6; Psalm 140:1; Isaiah 14:4; Ezekiel 21:25; and Zechariah 11:16–17.

The powerful and ominous figure we know as the Antichrist appears throughout Scripture under various names and guises. As you compare the descriptions of this man in the Old and New Testaments, you find a portrait of a powerful man of remarkable personal appeal and deceptive powers. He is called the "Antichrist," the "man of Lawlessness" (2 Thessalonians 2:3), the "beast" (Revelation 13), the "false shepherd" (Zechariah 11), and various other titles. He is a political ruler and the human incarnation of Satan on Earth. He is the one who will gather up in himself all the humanistic philosophies of the earth, receive the worship of all the nations of the earth, and set himself in opposition to the worship of the one true God.

Will the Temple Be Rebuilt?

If the temple was destroyed by Titus in AD 70, what is this holy place in which the Antichrist will appear? There can be only one answer: The temple of Jerusalem must be rebuilt. This is implied in Jesus' own words. He predicted the destruction of the temple in AD 70, and then He prophesied "the abomination that causes desolation" at some unspecified time after that. Clearly, Jesus is telling us that there will come a time when the Jews will repossess the temple area, and during that time, the temple will be reconstructed.

In view of this prophecy, it may well be that the most important event since the Resurrection was Israel's capture of Old Jerusalem during the miraculous Six-Day War of June 1967. That event marked the first time in 1,897 years (since AD 70) that the Jews were in control of the temple site. True, that site is still occupied by the Muslim shrine called the Dome of the Rock. The existence of that Islamic edifice presents a huge obstacle to the rebuilding of the temple.

But there is no other place it can be built. God decreed in the Old Testament that Jewish sacrifices can be offered there and nowhere else on earth.

Having won possession of Old Jerusalem and the temple site in 1967, will Israel maintain possession until this prophecy is fulfilled? It's hard to imagine how anything short of an Armageddon-like war could ever wrest that land away from Jewish control. Will the Jews overcome the obstacle of rebuilding the temple on a place now occupied by a Muslim holy place? Somehow, it will be done. As Jesus has said, "the Scripture cannot be broken" (John 10:35).

I am personally acquainted with a group of Jewish people in Israel who are seriously working on plans to rebuild the temple. They have made great progress toward their goal, yet much remains to be done before the temple can be rebuilt. Understand, these Jewish people are not seeking to rebuild the temple in order to fulfill the prophecies of Jesus or Daniel. They are motivated purely by a desire to restore the Jewish religion to its original forms and practices. These people are single-minded in their dedication to the purpose of rebuilding the temple. And the temple *will* be rebuilt under the terms of a covenant that Israel makes with the man of lawlessness, the Antichrist.

A Literal Event—A Specific Place

Jesus tells us, in effect, "When you see the man who fulfills the qualifications described in the book of Daniel, and when you see him sitting in the temple and claiming to be God, then you will know that the end of the age has arrived." Jesus is not speaking symbolically or metaphorically. He is speaking plainly and literally.

The Man of Lawlessness will take his place in the temple and there he will receive the worship of the world. It will be a literal event occurring in a specific spot on earth at a definite moment in time.

The prophecy of the seventy weeks in Daniel clearly indicates that a seven-year period yet remains to be inaugurated before the prophecy is fulfilled. Daniel's prophecy also declares that it is in the middle of those seven years that the Antichrist will desecrate the Jewish temple by his claim to be God. It is evident, therefore, that only the last three-and-one-half years of this seven-year period can properly be called "the end of the age."

You find this same time frame designated in a variety of ways in other parts of the Bible. In Revelation 13:5, the time frame is given as "forty-two months," which equals three-and-a-half years. In Daniel 7:25, the time frame is given as "a time, times, and half a time." Most scholars agree that this means "a year, two years, and half a year," which again totals three and a half years. In Revelation 12:6, the time frame is given as "1,260 days," which again equals three-and-a-half years. Daniel also refers to this period as "the time of the end" (Daniel 8:17–19).

But the sign of the desolating sacrilege does much more than mark the beginning of the end time. It *describes* the end time. The signs of Scripture are not intended to be milestones to mark off the calendar. Rather, they reveal the hidden principles of the time in which they appear.

For example, the Jews continually demanded that Jesus give them a sign that He was the Messiah. He said to them, "An evil and adulterous generation craves for a sign; and yet no sign shall be given to it but the sign of Jonah the prophet; for just as Jonah was three days and three nights in the belly of the sea monster, so shall the Son of Man be three days and three nights in the heart of the earth" (Matthew 12:39–40, NASB). His own burial and resurrection, then, was to be the sign. When that sign occurred they would understand the meaning of His coming.

The sign of the resurrection did not come at the beginning of His ministry; it came at the end—yet it dramatized and symbolized the meaning of His coming. It stands forever as a symbol of the new life He came to give, the new principle by which men and women are intended to live as new creations.

In the same way, the sign of the desolating sacrilege not only marks the beginning of the end of the age, it also denotes the character of this period of time. It is a time of horror, blasphemy, and sacrilege against God.

If we could learn to read life rightly, we would find that almost everything is a sign. God is continually illuminating the invisible forces behind human affairs so that we can see them as visible events—if we will only look at them the right way. As we observe the events that take place in the world, we can gain insight into what is going on behind the scenes. That is the secret behind all that exists in this material world.

All around us are objects made of matter. We see visible, material things—a table, a chair, a wall—and we can see and understand what it is made of. A given object may be made of metal, wood, plastic, concrete, or some other substance. But anyone who has a smattering of high-school science knows that what we see is not the whole story. That which we call "matter" is actually a visible manifestation of invisible forces.

There is the force of gravity, that invisible attraction that mass has for mass. There is the electromagnetic force, which acts between electrically charged particles, producing electricity, magnetism, and light. There is the strong nuclear force that binds neutrons and protons together in the core of each atom. And there is the weak nuclear force that causes subatomic particles to decay. The universe is what it is because of invisible forces. Though unseen, these forces control everything from the structure of an atom to the motion of galaxies.

Something similar to this occurs in the realm of human events as well as in the realm of matter and physics. When the event takes place that Jesus describes, and the man of lawlessness sits in the temple of God, it will be the result of invisible forces operating within human hearts. By the time the Antichrist takes power, humanity will have already enthroned itself in God's place. The day is coming, Jesus says, when the human race will be confirmed in the deadly mindset that we are our own god, and we do not need any other god. On that day, the words of the psalmist will be fulfilled:

> Why are the nations in an uproar
> > And the peoples devising a vain thing?
>
> The kings of the earth take their stand
> > And the rulers take counsel together
> Against the LORD and against His Anointed:
>
> "Let us tear their fetters apart
> > And cast away their cords from us!" (Psalm 2:1–3)

But that is also the day when God will laugh, says the Psalmist. He will say:

> "But as for Me, I have installed My King
> > Upon Zion, My holy mountain." . . .
> Do homage to the Son, lest He become angry,
> > and you perish in the way,
> For His wrath may soon be kindled.
> > How blessed are all who take refuge in Him!
> > > > (Psalm 2:6,12, NASB)

Zion, the holy mountain, symbolizes the human spirit. Our innermost being is the place God has chosen as the royal residence for His Holy Spirit. His goal for us is that we become what He intended us to be: the human expression of the divine life, the means by which the invisible God is made visible in human affairs. Tragically, that is the place where human beings have enthroned themselves! They have renounced God and rejected His authority. They declare that they have no God but the god of the self!

The philosophy of humanism has been with us in one form or another for centuries, but it will reach its selfish, lawless apex in the last day. The apostle Paul wrote, "For the mystery of lawlessness is already at work" (2 Thessalonians 2:7, NASB). The I-am-my-own-god philosophy was at work even in the first century—and it has been slowly, steadily sending out its tendrils into human society ever since.

The apostle John wrote, "For many deceivers have gone out into the world, those who do not acknowledge Jesus Christ as coming in the flesh. This is the deceiver and the antichrist" (2 John 7, NASB). Antichrist does not come among us with a bolt of lightning and a blast of thunder. Antichrist creeps up on us with subtle deception, infecting our minds and clouding our vision. The goal of Antichrist is to undermine us slowly and gradually, century after century, until all of history is brought to a crisis point. When that happens and the Antichrist is revealed to the world, then, Jesus says, we have a clear signal of the end of the age.

In our own day, the lie of humanism grows gradually more powerful and persuasive: *Worship yourself!* You can hear it on every side, in a thousand and one subtle variations—from magazines bearing the title *Self* to commercials that sell not only shampoo but self-worship with the slogan, "It costs more—but I'm worth it!"

And there are also some not-so-subtle variations to this message of self-worship. On one Internet Web site, a practicing satanist proudly states, "Satanism is my path, freeing me to push aside all moral and religious limitations that get in the way of true living. It is a life-giving philosophy that allows me to live my own way and be my own god." Clearly, this deceived satanist has accepted the oldest lie of all—the same lie with which the Serpent tempted Adam and Eve in the Garden of Eden: "You don't have to follow God's rules. You can be your own god and write your own rules!"

We hear this same lie repeated all around us in the books and magazines we read, on TV and radio, and in the boardroom and around the office water cooler: "You control your world! You decide your own destiny! Why not have it all?" The spirit of this age is sometimes expressed as narcissism: "I am all that matters! No one is more important than me!" Sometimes it is expressed as solipsism: "I am all that is. Everything else is illusion. There is only one thing that I *know* exists, and that is *me*. Therefore, I am god."

It is not that the world does not acknowledge a certain place for God—but it is usually a very *small* place. A little religion, a little bit of God, is all right—but let's not go overboard. If going to church and dropping a few coins in the collection plate makes you feel better, fine. But you should never let God get in the way of your ambitions or your pleasure or your wants. Human beings make the rules. We exist for our own glory—and anyone who says otherwise had better stay out of our way!

Streams in the Desert

In time, this infectious, self-worshiping attitude will demand a leader who personifies this worldview. As the end of the age approaches, this self-worshiping philosophy will find its ultimate expression in a man who will have an unquenchable desire to be worshiped by the entire world.

When this man appears, the world will be ready to follow him to the end. But what is that end? Listen again to the Son of God in His Olivet prophecy: "'the abomination that causes desolation,' spoken of through the prophet Daniel."

How do you depict desolation? Most would think of a desert, a wilderness with the eternal wind moaning in torment across barren sand. That kind of desolation describes many lives I've known—and perhaps it describes people you've known. We hear the stories all the time of men and women, and even children, who experience nothing but futility and barrenness in their lives. Why? Because of the abomination that causes desolation. Because of the abysmal lie that we can be our own gods, that we have adequate resources to satisfy our own lives, that the search for status, pleasure, and material things can meet the deepest needs of our hearts. It's all a lie—an abominable lie that produces lives of desolation.

Jesus saw all this as He looked out across centuries to come. It is little wonder that tears rolled down His face as He looked out over the rebellious city below, where already the abomination that causes desolation had begun its evil work. He wept over the stubborn city as He weeps over the stubborn hearts of men and women today.

Against this backdrop of increasing desolation, the gospel comes as glorious good news. Sensing the emptiness in the lives around Him, Jesus said, "If anyone is thirsty, let him come to me and drink" (John 7:37). Where do you find thirsty people? In the wilderness! And what is the solution to the thirst that strikes in the desert? A river! So, Jesus said, "Whoever believes in me, as the Scripture has said, streams of living water will flow from within him" (John 7:38). The solution for thirst in the desert is to find a running, flowing stream and to drink from it. Jesus has provided streams of living water that gush forth from the inner depths of thirsty souls, quenching not only our own thirst but the thirst of people around us.

Jesus is the answer—but many people reject that answer, preferring to live in the desert with their thirst. Why? It seems inconceivable that people would prefer thirst to satisfaction, the wilderness to the cool, clear, living water. Yet the reason people reject Jesus and the living water is really quite simple: Human pride. In order to drink from the living water, a person must bend down and dip his hand into the stream. Some people are unwilling to bend, unwilling to stoop down to receive the living water, unwilling to humble themselves and admit their need to drink. We do not like to acknowledge our dependency and helplessness. We resist that, and if we will not bend, we cannot drink. If we cannot drink, we cannot live. We will die—victims of our own foolish pride.

Those who humble themselves to receive the living water will drink and live. And they will not have just one cupful to drink—they will be lavished with an endless stream of living water. This is God's answer to the emptiness and futility that surrounds us. Though the parched desert of desolate human experience is all around us, we have found the streams of living water that flow through the desert and bring refreshment.

The world is growing darker, coarser, more unloving and unfeeling, more hostile and dangerous, and yes, more *desolate* as the age grows to a close. With each passing year, the sense of futility around us deepens. Yet through these darkening days, the gospel continues to offer its glorious invitation: "Thirsty one! Bend down, drink, and live." ◇

4

When the Dam Breaks

Matthew 24:21-22; 36-42

The Danish philosopher Søren Kierkegaard (1813–1855) told a parable describing his vision of the end of the world. Imagine a theater, he said, in which a variety show is playing. There are musical acts, dancers, magicians, comedians, acrobats—one amazing act after another. Each act receives thunderous applause from the audience.

Suddenly, the show is interrupted as the theater manager steps onto the stage. Speaking calmly, not wanting to panic his patrons, the manager says, "Ladies and gentlemen, I regret to inform you that the theater is on fire. Please get up and move in an orderly fashion to the exits. There is plenty of time for you all to leave safely, but please do so at once."

There is a moment of stunned silence—and then the audience breaks out in laughter and applause. The theater patrons believe it's an act! They think the manager is a comedian!

"No! You don't understand," the manager says. "There really is a fire! You must get up and leave the building immediately!"

The patrons laugh even more uproariously, and they applaud and cheer even more loudly. The manager tries again to warn the people, but they will not believe him. Even when smoke and flames appear at the back of the stage, the audience thinks it is merely done for effect. The manager sees he can do no more, so he runs off the stage and out of the building. The audience, meanwhile, hoots and cheers and claps in appreciation of the manager's "performance."

Seconds later, fire sweeps through the building, killing everyone inside.

Kierkegaard concluded his parable, saying, "And so will our age, I think, go down in fiery destruction to the applause of a crowded house of cheering spectators."

On this matter, I believe Kierkegaard is right. To the people around us, life is a variety show, a vast amusement, one amazing act after another. The people of the world applaud and laugh and enjoy the show, little suspecting that the theater—the world itself—is on fire. The whole place is destined to be consumed. The Old Testament prophets, the New Testament prophets, and the Lord Jesus Himself have all warned of the approaching end, of the consuming fire that is about to sweep through human history and human society. No unbelieving soul will escape this conflagration—yet the laughter, cheering, and applause continue. And it will continue—

Until the end of the age.

The End of the Age

We now focus in on the passage in the Olivet discourse where Jesus describes to His disciples the end of the age. The end will not be a single climactic event, but a chain of events. These events are the inevitable consequence of forces that have been at work in society throughout the whole course of this age.

The Scriptures agree that the "abomination that causes desolation" that our Lord refers to is a man—a man of world prominence who enters the rebuilt temple in the city of Jerusalem and claims the power and worship that is due to God alone. So serious and blasphemous is the act of this Man of Lawlessness that it precipitates the greatest crisis the world ever will face. Jesus says:

"For then there will be great distress, unequaled from the beginning of the world until now—and never to be equaled again. If those days had not been cut short, no one would survive, but for the sake of the elect those days will be shortened." (Matthew 24:21–22)

Many have found those words hard to believe. They clearly refer to an hour unlike anything else in history. Until recent times, it had been thought incredible that any event or cluster of events could ever create such horror, upheaval, death, and destruction as Jesus describes. But recent developments in the science of warfare and terrorism, coupled with a deeper understanding of threats to the environment and the possibilities for natural disaster, have made the Lord's "doomsday scenario" seem not only credible but increasingly likely.

Here are some of the possible threats to human existence, several of which could be part of the "great distress" that Jesus foresees: Worldwide economic collapse, such as galloping inflation, global depression, or a worldwide banking or stock market collapse. Worldwide energy shortages. Runaway population growth. Plague, either natural or genetically engineered (germ warfare). Famine. AIDS. Nuclear war. A global computer disaster. Ecological disaster, such as global warming. An asteroid or comet collision with the earth. Political collapse brought about by global terrorism.

The rise of the man of lawlessness will unleash a flood of hatred, crime, and murder throughout the world. We must remember that political leaders only express emotions and passions that already lurk in the hearts of the people, waiting for the right moment to surge forth. Adolph Hitler did not teach the Nazis to hate the Jews. He only gave voice to a hatred and resentment that was already in hundreds of thousands of hearts. In the same way, when this man of lawlessness takes his place in the temple of God, he will unleash a torrent of sin and death that is already present in millions of human hearts across the globe.

It is also important to understand that the man of lawlessness will not be revealed to the world until the time is ripe. Imagine if any human being were to stand before the world and say, "I am your God! Worship me!" Would he be believed and accepted? Absolutely not—at least, not yet. There are forces at work right now that restrain evil from making a full and open manifestation. Evil cannot take over as the dominant philosophy of the human race until these restraining forces are removed.

Jesus once compared the kingdom of heaven to a farmer who planted a field of wheat. But while the farmer slept, an enemy planted weeds in the field. So when the wheat sprouted, so did the weeds. The farmer's servants wanted to uproot the weeds, but the farmer said, "No, because while you are pulling the weeds, you may root up the wheat with them. Let both grow together until the harvest. At that time I will tell the harvesters: First collect the weeds and tie them in bundles to be burned; then gather the wheat and bring it into my barn" (Matthew 13:29–30).

Then Jesus proceeded to explain the meaning of the parable: The field is the world. The good seed stands for the children of God's kingdom. The enemy is the devil and the weeds are the devil's children. Finally, Jesus says, "The harvest is the end of the age, and the harvesters are angels" (Matthew 13:39). Until the end of the age, Jesus says, the wheat and the weeds, the good and the evil, grow up together. That is why we live in a world filled with so much good—

and so much evil. The dominant philosophy in this world is not evil, but good—though there is enough evil in the world to make us wonder if evil isn't winning! It is only when the harvest arrives at the end of the age that evil is let loose to dominate the earth.

Evil Under Restraint

There's a limerick, author unknown, that expresses the way most of us feel about the relative balance of good and evil in the world:

Our race had an excellent beginning,
But man spoiled his chances by sinning.
    We hope that the story
    Will end in God's glory,
But at present the other side's winning!

It seems to many that evil is triumphant in our day. But no football team ever claimed victory based on the score at halftime. No baseball team was ever declared the winner during the seventh-inning stretch. The only score that matters is the final score. The great hymn, "This Is My Father's World," contains these lines of reassurance:

This is my Father's world.
    O let me ne'er forget
That though the wrong seems oft so strong,
    God is the ruler yet.

Despite widespread injustice and the terrible prevalence of violence and crime, the scales have not been tipped in favor of the wrong. The proof of this fact is that evil must constantly disguise itself as good in order to survive. Swindlers try to appear respectable. Prostitutes want to be called "ladies." Tyrants must pose as benefactors. Liars always strive to appear truthful.

Only the good is really acceptable. Evil must dissemble and disguise itself to gain acceptance. Once evil is unmasked, it is rejected by the world. This fact alone is ample proof that even the massive power of evil that we see on every hand is still held in check by the even more massive power of good.

Evil continually breaks out in the form of cruelty and violence, corruption and depravity. It crops up in the lives of individuals, in homes and corporations and nations, but evil is always beaten back, overpowered, and subdued again. Individual human beings may live in open rebellion and complete depravity—but they also live in guilt. People know that they need God. Some, in their hour of need, will seek Him and find Him.

Evil is powerful, but hemmed in by forces of good. This accounts for the naive optimism of many who profess faith in "human goodness." In their pollyannish blindness, they claim that human beings are "basically good," and they reject the biblical revelation that goodness stems from the kindness of God on our behalf. They ignore the biblical truth that human beings, though made in God's good image and likeness, are hopelessly marred by sin and rebellion. Our fundamental nature is corrupted. That is why there is only one hope for our redemption: the sacrifice of Jesus, who died in our place.

When the Restraints are Removed

Jesus reveals the truth. At the end of the age, He says, the nature of spiritual and social reality will be suddenly, radically changed. Evil will reign in triumph. All bonds will be broken, all restraints cast aside. Lawlessness will fill the earth. God will move in judgment, terrible catastrophes will sweep the earth, but men and women will stubbornly refuse to repent. Fear will not drive humanity to prayer but to further defiance. The human race will not wish to be delivered but only to be destroyed. People will take no delight in good but will celebrate the triumph of evil.

The prophecy of Jesus is affirmed by three vivid pictures from the book of Revelation. The larger part of that book traces the course of events in the Great Tribulation. It especially reveals the condition of human hearts during that time of worldwide crisis. The first picture from Revelation shows the stubborn, willful spirit of unrepentance in that time.

> The rest of mankind that were not killed by these plagues still did not repent of the work of their hands; they did not stop worshiping demons, and idols of gold, silver, bronze, stone and wood—idols that cannot see or hear or walk. Nor did they repent of their murders, their magic arts, their sexual immorality or their thefts. (Revelation 9:20–21)

The second picture from Revelation depicts the fear men experience, coupled with a stubborn preference for destruction over repentance and salvation.

> I watched as he opened the sixth seal. There was a great earthquake. The sun turned black like sackcloth made of goat hair, the whole moon turned blood red, and the stars in the sky fell to earth, as late figs drop from a fig tree when shaken by a strong wind. The sky receded like a scroll, rolling up, and every mountain and island was removed from its place.
>
> Then the kings of the earth, the princes, the generals, the rich, the mighty, and every slave and every free man hid in caves and among the rocks of the mountains. They called to the mountains and the rocks, "Fall on us and hide us from the face of him who sits on the throne and from the wrath of the

Lamb! For the great day of their wrath has come, and who can stand?" (Revelation 6:12–17)

The third picture from Revelation is probably the most heart-stopping and horrifying of all.

> Now when they have finished their testimony, the beast that comes up from the Abyss will attack them, and over-power and kill them. Their bodies will lie in the street of the great city, which is figuratively called Sodom and Egypt, where also their Lord was crucified. For three and a half days men from every people, tribe, language and nation will gaze on their bodies and refuse them burial. The inhabitants of the earth will gloat over them and will celebrate by sending each other gifts, because these two prophets had tormented those who live on the earth. (Revelation 11:7–10)

Clearly, the character of that time is very different from the character of the times in which we now live. Chronologically speaking, the end of the age may not be very far off—but in terms of the spirit that characterizes that age, it is a world removed from our own, an alien world operating on alien principles of absolute evil. We are drawing nearer to that sort of world all the time. We see stirrings and outbreaks of incredible evil—but as yet, we have not reached the point where all of society, all across the globe, takes a blatant, unblushing delight in evil.

One thing is certain: There must be some future event that forms the dividing line between our time and that time. There must be some event we can point to in the outline of future history that produces this astounding change in human society. What is the event that triggers this global reign of evil?

Perhaps it would be better to put the question another way: What is it that now *restrains* evil?

The clue is found in the Sermon on the Mount in Matthew 5. There, Jesus says some amazing things to the little band of disciples gathered around Him. Remember, these were ordinary men—fishermen, tax collectors, farmers, and political rabble-rousers, most of them poorly educated—yet He says to them, "You are the salt of the earth. . . . You are the light of the world" (Matthew 5:13–14).

What did Jesus mean? He meant that the disciples were light because they had the life of Jesus living in them. As the gospel of John tells us, "In him was life, and that life was the light of men" (John 1:4). Human lives give off light only when they are in touch with the life that comes from Jesus Christ. Here were men—simple, ordinary men—who possessed *life*. And because they had life, their lives shone with light.

Moreover, they were salt, because they had savor. Jesus spoke of salt which is without savor and good for nothing. Men will cast savorless salt out and tread it under their feet. But here were men who had savor, a unique and different flavor. The life they possessed, the life of Jesus Christ, made them different. It gave them a different kind of character. It made them a different kind of people. They had a different light on their faces and a different reason for living. They had a different authority in their lives and a different power than other men.

Salt doesn't merely add savor to food. It is also a preservative, halting the process of corruption. Meat that might spoil in a matter of hours can be salted and either dried or kept in brine and preserved for months. That is the preserving power of salt. So Jesus said that His disciples were as salt that pervaded society, molding human thought, challenging evil, restraining, controlling, limiting, binding, resisting the malignancy of sin in human affairs.

This is why Christians must not isolate themselves from society. They must not retreat into mountaintop monasteries. They must not form walled-off, gated Christian communities that are set apart from the world. Christians must put on their hip-boots and wade into the muck and mire of human misery. Christians must go where the sinners are, just as their Lord did, and they must serve and love sinners. Christians must show sinners the way to the One who loved them and died for them. And Christians must permeate every aspect of life, every level of society, with the light of truth.

Christians are salt, but salt is of no value while it remains in the salt shaker.

A Secret Revealed

When Paul wrote to the Thessalonian Christians about the coming of the lawless one, he said, "And now you know what is holding him back, so that he may be revealed at the proper time" (2 Thessalonians 2:6). The Thessalonians were aware of the restraining force that held evil in check in their own time. They had only to look into their own lives to see what restrained the lawlessness within their own hearts and minds. They knew, as we also know, that the "sinful nature desires what is contrary to the Spirit, and the Spirit what is contrary to the sinful nature. They are in conflict with each other" (Galatians 5:17).

Who or what restrains evil in the life of a Christian? The Holy Spirit, of course. That is the glorious secret that Paul calls "Christ in you, the hope of glory," the life of Jesus, imparted by the Holy Spirit, acting as a barrier and a restraint against the manifestation of evil.

As Paul told the Thessalonians, "For the secret power of lawlessness is already at work; but the one who now holds it back will continue to do so till he is taken out of the way. And then the lawless one will be revealed" (2 Thessalonians 2:7–8). All restraints must be removed before the man of lawlessness, the Antichrist, can be fully revealed. All restraints must be removed before it becomes visible to the whole world what depths of evil are in human beings who live totally apart from God. The salt must be taken out of society in order for the rottenness to become evident. When the restraints are removed, the arrogant pride of humanity will break out into the open as the Antichrist steps forth and claims to be God.

At that moment, the powers of darkness will be set free and the dark night of judgment will begin. "For then there will be great distress," Jesus says, "unequaled from the beginning of the world until now—and never to be equaled again" (Matthew 24:21).

When will the restraining, preserving "salt" be removed from our society? If we hope to tie it to some specific date on the calendar, we are doomed to disappointment. Jesus continually warned against any attempt to set dates. But we *can* know the time of this removal in relation to other events at the close of the age.

Since Paul says plainly that the Holy Spirit will be taken out of the world before the Antichrist is revealed, we know that His removal from the world occurs somewhere between the events recorded in Matthew 24:14 and the events of verse 15. It will occur sometime before the "abomination that causes desolation," spoken of by the prophet Daniel, stands in the holy place of the restored temple. Here is that event, as placed within the context of the Olivet discourse in Matthew 24:

> Verse 14: "And this gospel of the kingdom will be preached in the whole world as a testimony to all nations, and then the end will come." [The Holy Spirit, present in the lives of Christians, is suddenly removed from the world. All restraints against evil are suddenly lifted.]

Verse 15: "So when you see standing in the holy place 'the abomination that causes desolation,' spoken of through the prophet Daniel—"

How long will it be from the time the restraining Holy Spirit is removed until "the abomination that causes desolation" is revealed? No one knows. Many Bible scholars feel there will be at least three and a half years between the removal of the Holy Spirit and the revelation of "the abomination that causes desolation." In other words, they say that the Holy Spirit will be removed from the earth at the beginning of the seven-year period that is Daniel's seventieth week. This would allow some time for the corruption of society to take place. It would allow for a mindset of evil to spread and entrench itself, ultimately producing a worldwide delight in the blasphemies of the man of lawlessness when he is revealed in the temple. When all references in Scripture to this event are taken into consideration, this seems to be the most likely time for the great removal to occur.

How will it take place? By what means is the Holy Spirit taken out of the way so that evil is permitted to run rampant? From many Scriptures the answer comes: The church will suddenly be taken out of the world! This does not mean the organized, institutional church. It means the *true* church, consisting of Christians in all denominations (and Christians who belong to no denomination at all) who possess the indwelling life of Jesus Christ. As we have already seen, it is through such Christians that the Holy Spirit exercises His restraining work in society. So to remove the Christians is to remove the Holy Spirit, along with the restraints that now hold evil in check.

Does Jesus say anything about the removal of His church from the world? Yes. In fact, He says so here in the Olivet discourse! He does not mention it at the time it occurs chronologically (between verses 14 and 15), but He does describe the event in verses 36–42:

> "No one knows about that day or hour, not even the angels in heaven, nor the Son, but only the Father. As it was in the days of Noah, so it will be at the coming of the Son of Man. For in the days before the flood, people were eating and drinking, marrying and giving in marriage, up to the day Noah entered the ark; and they knew nothing about what would happen until the flood came and took them all away. That is how it will be at the coming of the Son of Man. Two men will be in the field; one will be taken and the other left. Two women will be grinding with a hand mill; one will be taken and the other left.
>
> "Therefore keep watch, because you do not know on what day your Lord will come." (Matthew 24:36–42)

Jesus introduces this event with a warning: No one knows the day or hour, and it is foolishness to tie this event to any specific date. We are not to try to figure out the timetable of God's program for history. Our assignment as followers of Christ is simply to be faithful and watchful every hour of every day, until either the moment of death or the moment Jesus takes us out of the world.

We must understand that when Jesus speaks about His return, He is not referring to a single moment of time when He will appear. Rather, He is talking about a return that covers a period of time. It will begin with a secret arrival, when He will come like a thief in the night. This will be the beginning of His "presence," the *parousia.*[1]

That presence will continue throughout all the time of trouble on earth, but it will be a behind-the-scenes presence, invisible to the world. Then, after the terrible upheaval and distress of those days (the Great Tribulation), He will manifest His presence visibly, appearing in power and great glory.

The invisible presence of Jesus on earth is not something new. During the forty days after His resurrection, He was present in exactly this way. He appeared and disappeared among His disciples and they never knew when He was coming or when He would leave. He was suddenly there, and just as suddenly gone. When He was not visibly present, He was here but not here. For forty days, this manifestation of Jesus went on until He ascended into heaven. When He comes again, He will resume the same relationship to the believing Jews and Gentiles of that time. The church will be caught up to be with Him, to join Him in that remarkable presence during the terrible days of trouble on earth.

The Removal of the Church

The removal of the church is described in various passages of Scripture. Paul writes to the Thessalonians about it in this passage:

> According to the Lord's own word, we tell you that we who are still alive, who are left till the coming [*parousia*] of the Lord, will certainly not precede those who have fallen asleep [that is, those who have died]. For the Lord himself will come down from heaven, with a loud command, with the voice of the archangel and with the trumpet call of God, and the dead in Christ will rise first. After that, we who are still alive and are left will be caught up together with them in the clouds to meet the Lord in the air. And so we will be with the Lord forever. Therefore encourage each other with these words. (1 Thessalonians 4:15–18)

The event Paul describes is the departure of the church. Another term often used for this event is the Rapture of the church—the event when the church is "caught up" or "raptured" into the clouds to meet the Lord Jesus in the air. The word *rapture* comes from the Latin word *rapiemur*, which is used in the Latin Vulgate translation of 1 Thessalonians 4:17, where Paul says that "we who are still alive and are left will be caught up [*rapiemur*] together with them in the clouds to meet the Lord in the air."

The message of the coming departure of the church is, as Paul says, a source of great comfort to Christians. It is called in Titus 2:13 "the blessed hope." It means that one whole generation of Christians will not physically die but will pass directly into a glorified state, as Jesus did on the Mount of Transfiguration before the astonished eyes of Peter, James, and John (see Matthew 17:2). No wonder one Christian said, "I'm not waiting for the undertaker; I'm waiting for the uppertaker!"

It would be easy for us to get carried away, imagining what this event will be like. But it is unlikely that this event will be visible to the world. It will be unseen and unfelt, with no disturbance of graves and nothing to indicate that anything has happened other than the strange disappearance of thousands of people. Just as the body of Jesus Christ was raised from the dead and passed out through the tomb without any physical manifestation, so will this event be. At the Resurrection, the stone was not rolled away to let Jesus out but to let the disciples see in! The removal of the church from the world will also be a silent event, unnoticed by the world. Here is how Paul describes that event:

> Listen, I tell you a mystery: We will not all sleep, but we will all be changed—in a flash, in the twinkling of an eye, at the last trumpet. For the trumpet will sound, the dead will be

raised imperishable, and we will be changed. (1 Corinthians 15:51–52)

The whole point of our Lord's revelation of this fantastic event is summed up in these words from the Olivet discourse: "Therefore keep watch, because you do not know on what day your Lord will come." Do not be deceived. Do not be swept off your feet by the satanic propaganda of this age. Don't become infected by the mind-set of this dying world.

The great removal of the church could take place at any moment. Are you waiting? Are you watching? ◇

5

God's Plan for Israel

Matthew 24:16–20

Two sisters, one thirteen years old and the other fourteen, were very close. They shared a bedroom, they shared their belongings, they went everywhere together, and they did everything together. There was only one thing they didn't share: Faith.

Laura, the thirteen-year-old, had a sweet, trusting faith in Jesus Christ. Susan, the fourteen-year-old, didn't believe in Jesus. She was a little on the wild side. She liked her fun and didn't want "religion" to get in the way of a good time.

One day Laura persuaded Susan to go with her to a church service. The minister preached from Matthew 24, the Olivet discourse, in which Jesus described how He would come for His own. Those who believed in Him would be taken; those who didn't believe would be left. It was a powerful sermon, and Laura was sure that her sister Susan would finally be moved to receive Jesus as her Lord and Savior.

But after the service, Susan seemed to be completely untouched by the message! Laura was heartbroken. She worried that Susan might never respond to the gospel.

That night, Laura and Susan climbed into their beds. "Susan," Laura said, "don't you ever wonder what would happen to you if Jesus returned and—"

"Goodnight, Laura," Susan said, ending the discussion before it began. She turned out the light, rolled over, and went to sleep.

But Laura couldn't sleep. She tossed and turned and prayed that God would reveal the truth to her sister. After an hour of insomnia, Laura got up to get a glass of milk from the kitchen.

While Laura was gone, Susan woke up and looked around. "Laura?" she said. When there was no answer, Susan turned on the light by her bedside and saw that Laura's bed was empty.

Oh, no! Susan thought. *It really happened! Jesus came and took Laura—and I've been left behind!*

Susan began to weep and pray, pleading with God for salvation—and that's when Laura returned and found Susan in a near-hysterical state. The girls prayed together, and Susan became a believer.

Someday, many people will experience what Laura's sister Susan experienced for a few moments—the terror of being left behind, the awful emptiness of knowing that they have made a disastrous choice. Even so, those who are left behind after the removal of God's church are not without hope. They are not beyond the reach of God's grace. Even though God will take the church out of the world before the Great Tribulation begins, those who are left will still have a chance to know God—though the challenge of living as a Christian in an antichristian world will be unbelievably hard!

That is the theme we will explore in this section of the Olivet discourse.

The Terror That Is Coming to Jerusalem

We return again to the words of Jesus to His disciples on the Mount of Olives. After announcing the sign of the close of the age as "the abomination that causes desolation" in the holy place of the temple, Jesus adds:

> "Then let those who are in Judea flee to the mountains. Let no one on the roof of his house go down to take anything out of the house. Let no one in the field go back to get his cloak. How dreadful it will be in those days for pregnant women and nursing mothers! Pray that your flight will not take place in winter or on the Sabbath." (Matthew 24:16–20)

Who are these words of Jesus addressed to? Who are the ones who must flee when the last days begin? Who are the people who evacuate so quickly that they dare not go back even for an overcoat? The answer is obvious, for Jesus tells us plainly, "those who are in Judea." This is not a symbolic or metaphorical passage. Jesus is telling us what will happen in a specific geographic region. Judea is part of ancient Palestine and present-day Israel. It comprises the city of Jerusalem and the hill country surrounding the city. Jesus addresses this warning specifically to the residents of Jerusalem and Judea.

Moreover, the Lord's mention of the Sabbath establishes the fact that these Judean residents are practicing, religious Jews. He urges them to pray that their flight will not be in the winter, with the physical distress of cold weather, or on the Sabbath, when Jews are under religious travel restrictions. In Matthew 24:22, Jesus calls these Jews "the elect" ("for the sake of the elect those days will be shortened"). This makes it clear that they are *believing* Jews—men and women who know and love Jesus Christ as Lord and are prepared to live and die for Him.

It is interesting that these Jewish Christians still observe the Jewish Sabbath, since Christians, according to the teaching of the New Testament epistles, are free from the Jewish law and no longer

observe special days, feasts, new moons, and Sabbaths. In his letter
to the Colossians, Paul writes:

> Therefore do not let anyone judge you by what you eat
> or drink, or with regard to a religious festival, a New Moon
> celebration or a Sabbath day. These are a shadow of the things
> that were to come; the reality, however, is found in Christ.
> (Colossians 2:16–17)

The apostle Paul clearly speaks of the Sabbath as a "shadow"
that will be superseded by Christ, who is the reality. Yet the Sabbath, Jesus says, will be a restricting factor in the flight of the Jewish Christians from Judea. Here, then, is a class of people who
cannot be identified with the present-day church. They are Jewish
believers in Christ who will be converted after the removal of the
church and before the time of the Great Tribulation.

This fact raises a problematical question: How will these Jews
become believers in Christ, since there are no Christians left to
preach the gospel after the removal of the church? In the description Paul gives of the departure of the church, we find the hint of
an answer. He writes:

> For the Lord himself will come down from heaven, with
> a loud command, with the voice of the archangel and with
> the trumpet call of God, and the dead in Christ will rise first.
> (1 Thessalonians 4:16)

Notice that the Lord Jesus will descend from heaven accompanied by three remarkable sounds: (1) a "loud command," or shout;
(2) the voice of the archangel, and (3) the sounding of the trumpet of God. Why are these three sounds important?

The shout comes from the Lord Himself. As He appears to the
church, He will call with a loud voice. This reminds us of the moment

when He stood before the tomb of Lazarus and called with a great voice, "Lazarus! Come forth!" Some Bible scholars believe that if He had not specifically said, "Lazarus," the entire cemetery would have emptied! The great shouted command of the Lord is literally a shout to wake the dead. Jesus Himself said in John 5:28–29, "Do not be amazed at this, for a time is coming when all who are in their graves will hear his voice [the voice of the Son of God] and come out."

And what of the trumpet? The trumpet of God is used throughout Scripture as a call to assemble. In fact, that is the universal function of a trumpet. In the Roman army, the trumpet blast signaled the start of a march. In the wilderness, Moses summoned the people of Israel to begin their journey with the sound of a trumpet. While the shout of the Lord summons the dead, the trumpet of the Lord summons the living. After the dead in Christ have been awakened by the shout of the Lord, Paul says, "we who are still alive and are left will be caught up together with them in the clouds to meet the Lord in the air. And so we will be with the Lord forever" (1 Thessalonians 4:17). The trumpet will sound the beginning of that great gathering of the church.

And what of the archangel's voice? Scripture refers only to one archangel. His name is Michael. He appears a number of times in the Bible and always in connection with the people of Israel. He is mentioned in Daniel 12, where Daniel is told:

> At that time Michael, the great prince who protects your people, will arise. There will be a time of distress such as has not happened from the beginning of nations until then. But at that time your people—everyone whose name is found written in the book—will be delivered. (Daniel 12:1)

The archangel, Michael, is called "the great prince" who protects the people of Daniel, the Jewish people. It is strongly suggested here that Michael, the great archangel, is responsible for opening the eyes of certain Jews living in Judea at the time of the departure of the church, and that they will recognize the Lord Jesus as their true Messiah. These Jewish people will then place their trust in Jesus as their Lord and Savior.

The 144,000 from the Twelve Tribes

We may link this passage with one in the book of Revelation, where there is a description of an event that seems remarkably similar, if not identical, to the event in Daniel 12. The apostle John writes:

> Then I saw another angel coming up from the east, having the seal of the living God. He called out in a loud voice to the four angels who had been given power to harm the land and the sea: "Do not harm the land or the sea or the trees until we put a seal on the foreheads of the servants of our God." Then I heard the number of those who were sealed: 144,000 from all the tribes of Israel. (Revelation 7:2–4)

Here a great angel undertakes a special task connected with Israel. He is not called an archangel, though he might be Michael. The 144,000 believers who are sealed are clearly Jewish believers, for the passage clearly states that they come from all the tribes of Israel. The passage goes on to list the twelve tribes of Israel and to declare that 12,000 are chosen from each tribe. Further information is given concerning this special group in Revelation:

> Then I looked, and there before me was the Lamb, standing on Mount Zion, and with him 144,000 who had his name and his Father's name written on their foreheads. . . . And they sang a new song before the throne and before the four living

creatures and the elders. No one could learn the song except the 144,000 who had been redeemed from the earth. These are those who did not defile themselves with women, for they kept themselves pure. They follow the Lamb wherever he goes. They were purchased from among men and offered as firstfruits to God and the Lamb. (Revelation 14:1, 3–4)

The book of Revelation goes on to describe the Great Tribulation as "the hour of his [God's] judgment" (Revelation 14:7). Before that hour arrives, these 144,000 believers from the tribes of Israel will be seen with the Lamb on Mount Zion. This is a specific location within the city limits of Jerusalem. The Revelation account confirms the fact that Jesus Christ will be on earth during this time and will reveal Himself from time to time to these Jewish disciples, just as He appeared to His followers during those remarkable forty days after His resurrection.

These 144,000 Jews are to be turned from unbelief to belief in much the same dramatic way as the apostle Paul was converted on the road to Damascus. Paul was thunderstruck by the sudden appearance of the risen Lord Jesus Christ. Paul speaks of himself in 1 Corinthians 15:8 as "one abnormally born," as one who was born in an extraordinary way, at an extraordinary time. He may have thought of himself as properly belonging to this special band of future Jewish believers, and felt that, by the grace of God, he had been born ahead of time and was given the privilege of belonging to the church.

Israel Revisited

Having seen the Lord Jesus with their own eyes, having stood with Him on Mount Zion, these 144,000 Jewish believers will be like

144,000 apostle Pauls, proclaiming the eternal gospel in mighty Spirit-given power throughout the whole earth. During this time, the lawless one will be moving to consolidate his power and to present himself to the world as God. The visible appearance of Christ to the 144,000 is the beginning of the fulfillment of God's renewed activity with the Jews, long predicted by the Old Testament prophets.

Paul also says that, despite the centuries of wandering following the destruction of the temple in Jerusalem, God will not cast off His people. He will call them back again and renew a relationship with them. In Romans chapter 11, Paul warns that we Gentiles must never assume that God has set aside the nation of Israel, for all the promises He has made to them will be fulfilled. Because of unbelief, Paul says, God scattered them around the earth and opened the door of blessing to all nations without distinction.

But the Gentiles, too, will fail God, as did the Jews. They too will be set aside, and God will call Israel back into national blessing. That is the work He will begin with the calling of the 144,000. Will anyone believe the message these 144,000 proclaim? If they do, it will be at the risk of their lives because the man of lawlessness, the Antichrist, will soon be in full control—and he will not allow worship to be given to anyone but himself. As the apostle John writes:

> After this I looked and there before me was a great multitude that no one could count, from every nation, tribe, people and language, standing before the throne and in front of the Lamb. They were wearing white robes and were holding palm branches in their hands. And they cried out in a loud voice:
>
> "Salvation belongs to our God,
>   who sits on the throne,
> and to the Lamb." . . .

> Then one of the elders asked me, "These in white robes—who are they, and where did they come from?"
>
> I answered, "Sir, you know." And he said, "These are they who have come out of the great tribulation; they have washed their robes and made them white in the blood of the Lamb." (Revelation 7:9–10, 13–14)

This multitude of Gentiles will be converted at the eleventh hour of history, evidently as a result of hearing and believing the gospel preached by the 144,000 believers of Israel sent by the Son of God. The greater part of the Gentile multitude will likely be martyred for their faith. In other parts of Revelation, we are told that many will be put to death because they will not worship the beast (the Antichrist) or his image.

Though they will indeed be "a great multitude," as John said, it is evident that they will be different in one remarkable way from the present-day church: They will not exercise the ministry of salt. They will have no preserving or restraining effect upon the society around them. They will be the light of the world, exposing (and thus condemning) the evil of the world, but they will not be able to influence the world toward good. The corruption will be too widespread for this believing multitude to turn back the evil tide. Those who speak the truth will be a tiny minority standing against a world completely given over to lies and a strong delusion.

Because there will be no salt at work in that society of the future, the dark menace of human arrogance will grow even more wildly conceited. Like the Sorcerer's Apprentice, science will go blithely on, mixing evil potions and conjuring up ever more frightening inventions of uncontrollable power. Human beings already believe that anything that can be done is permissible, for there are no moral boundaries in a world that has dismissed God. If we want to create artificial human beings, why shouldn't we? If we want to engineer disease organisms that have never existed before, what is to stop us? If we choose to completely reshape nature and even redefine what it means to be human, who can tell us "No"? God? What God? *We* are God!

In our arrogance and ignorance, we have tipped the delicate balance of nature. Like an intoxicated man in a rocking canoe, we don't even realize that the next drunken lurch could overturn everything and drown us.

The apostle Peter tells us that all of this has happened before. There was a time when human beings, in arrogance and pride, boasting of the civilization they had built, unwittingly tripped the lever that held the world in delicate balance. Before those people knew what they had brought upon themselves, the clouds gathered, the sky darkened, the heavens poured down floods of water, the earth heaved, the seas rose up over the mountaintops, and the world of humankind perished—

Except for eight souls who were safely preserved in an ark of wood.

Here again, in the Olivet discourse, Jesus tells us that the human race—so clever, yet so insanely arrogant—will again go too far. The sign of it will be a world gone mad with self-conceit, a world committed to the proposition that there is no God in the universe, and that human beings are their own god and need no other. Then the deadly lever will be tripped by humanity's own hand.

What form will the ultimate destruction take? The dark forces of nature will be released—perhaps as a result of humanity's conceited and overconfident tampering with nature. Perhaps the seals of nuclear power will be removed, and a firestorm of searing radiation will sweep the globe. Perhaps vials of mutated biological organisms will be poured out upon the earth. In any case, we know from reading the book of Revelation that there will be calamity, death, fire, plague, and destruction on a scale that has never been visited upon humanity before.

Light in the Darkness

At this point, you may be thinking that this is a grim picture of the future—and indeed, it is! Isn't there any ray of comfort and light to shine through these storm clouds of prophecy? Yes, there is. In fact, there are three rays of light to encourage us as we face the full implications of this remarkable prophecy of Jesus.

The first ray of light: The midnight hour has not yet arrived. We may be near, very near, but the hour of God's grace has not yet expired. I am not attempting to frighten anyone into believing in Jesus Christ. I am simply stating that it is wise to face what Jesus Himself has said. He told us that He came into the world not to condemn it but to save. Jesus is not interested in beating men over the head with a billy club of prophecy.

But Jesus came into the world, John 1:14 tells us, "full of grace and truth." He has given us grace—but He has also given us truth, the prophetic truth of the Olivet discourse. Jesus came to give us new life, but He has also told us what life is like apart from Him: we are helpless and doomed without Him, and condemned to destruction. So with His grace comes His warning, and the grace cannot save us unless we heed the warning.

This long-range prediction of the Lord's is uncannily, compellingly aligned with the present trend of world events. So this prediction should awaken us to the reality that lies ahead of the human race. It forces us to confront the questions: What are we living for? Are we spending our lives in a quest for something that will be

swept away in the fires of the Great Tribulation? Or are we investing our lives in a lasting relationship with the Lord throughout eternity? We cannot have it both ways. We must choose one or the
other.

The second ray of light: God's dealings with Israel, as revealed in
this prophecy, mirror His dealings with us as believers. We often see
this principle in Scripture: God's relationship to Israel is frequently
a metaphor to describe His relationship to individual Christians.
Notice these parallels:

As a nation, Israel has long lived in unbelief toward the Lord
Jesus Christ. The people of Israel have wandered in obscurity and
persecution for centuries. Any Christian knows that there are also
times of unbelief in his own life. Though he is a believer, at times
he can be a very unbelieving believer. The result of those times of
unbelief is a feeling of wandering, of being lost in the dark, and distant from God.

But this account of the 144,000 Jewish believers shows how
God can break through unbelief. He can bring the light of Jesus
streaming through the darkness just when we need it most. You
may be going through a crisis experience right now. God is about
to bring new light into your heart so that you will no longer walk
in barrenness and darkness, but in light, glory, and peace.

The key to deliverance is to accept not only the light but the
darkness as from God. When we can thank Him for the darkness,
then the light is not far away. That is what will eventually happen
to Israel, and it is what God is waiting to bring about for us now.

The third ray of light: Everything is happening on schedule and
according to God's sovereign plan. It has all been anticipated and
predicted. Perhaps the most comforting word Jesus ever spoke to
His disciples is found in John 14:1–2: "Do not let your hearts be
troubled. Trust in God; trust also in me. In my Father's house [the

universe] are many rooms [places to live; earth is one of these rooms, but there are others]; if it were not so, I would have told you. I am going there to prepare a place for you." That is a comforting word indeed!

Jesus came to set the record straight, to correct our misunderstandings, and to reveal the outline of future history for us so that we can know the truth. These strange and frightening events He has foretold will certainly come to pass—and when they do, they will not be a surprise to God. He has seen the end from the beginning. Even the time of the Great Tribulation is fully known to Him—and God has promised that the Tribulation will not be the end of the story.

Beyond the darkness lies the dawn of a new day for this weary, suffering, beaten world. As people of faith, we lift up our eyes, we strengthen our hearts, and we rejoice. Let the future come. We have no fear.

Our God is in control. ◇

6

Russia, Religion, and Ruin

Matthew 7:21–23; Revelation 17:1–6

Louis XI (1423–83) was the king of France—but the people called him The Spider. Some say his nickname was the result of his physical ugliness; others say it was because of his spider-like skill at spinning invisible webs of political intrigue in which he caught and destroyed his opponents. His cruel, efficient reign was marked by bribery, treachery, and repression.

The Spider was a devout believer in astrology. His faith in astrology was strengthened when one of the forecasts of his court astrologer, Galeotti Martivalle, seemed to come true. After a lady of the king's court died, Galeotti matched the circumstances of the woman's death to a vaguely worded prediction he had made the previous week. In this way, he convinced King Louis that he had accurately forecast the woman's death.

Having this "prophet" around made The Spider nervous. What if Galeotti didn't merely *predict* the woman's death? What if he actually *caused* it by some sort of magic spell? The Spider decided to dispose of the astrologer—just to be safe.

So King Louis told a few of his trusted servants, "I shall summon Galeotti to my chamber in the high tower. When I give you the signal, seize him and throw him out the window to his death."

Then the court astrologer was summoned. When Galeotti arrived at the king's chamber in the high tower, he sensed something was amiss. The king's servants eyed Galeotti strangely, and The Spider himself seemed fidgety and anxious.

"I am quite impressed," the king began, "that you were able to foretell the death of that woman. You seem to know much about the fate of others. Tell me—do you know what your fate will be, and how long you have to live?"

"I only know," Galeotti said, thinking quickly, "that I shall die just three days before Your Majesty."

The king considered Galeotti's reply—then he canceled his plans to murder the astrologer.

Predictions can be frightening and disturbing! The prophecies in the Olivet discourse certainly fall into that category. Many people who read the Lord's predictions about the end of the age are deeply troubled that these prophecies are so eerily aligned with events in the world today. It wouldn't be a problem if the Lord's prophecies were stated in sweeping generalities and ambiguous symbols—so much sound and fury, signifying nothing. But it is alarming to read biblical prophecy as specific and detailed as the Olivet discourse.

Some people would rather turn to a less threatening passage—the Sermon on the Mount, say, or some of the Lord's less troubling parables. But all this talk of the Great Tribulation—they want nothing of it. To these people, the prophecies of the Olivet discourse seem like strange, out-of-character words for Jesus to speak—but that is because they do not understand who Jesus truly is. The truth is that Jesus speaks as openly and freely about the Antichrist and the Great Tribulation as He talks of forgiveness and love. He clearly regards the prophecies of the Old Testament in the most literal terms, adding His own predictions in straightforward, unambiguous language.

Once you realize that Jesus is the Lord of history and the Supreme Judge of humankind, you recognize the Olivet discourse as the centerpiece of all that Jesus says and does. Through the lens of this prophecy, we catch a glimpse of God's great purpose in human history.

Two Powers—Political and Religious

In this chapter we meet two forces that are powerfully at work during the close of the age but which are not specifically mentioned by Jesus in the Olivet discourse. Our Lord attempts to give only a general outline of the events of that time, and we must look to parallel passages of Scripture to find the details. Jesus indicates that the Antichrist will exercise worldwide power at the time of the Great Tribulation. But there is no specific mention of two other powers present during a portion of that time. These two powers must be removed before the Antichrist can reign unopposed. One is a political power; the other is a religious power.

The political power is Russia. The religious rival is the false institutional church that remains behind after the true church has been removed. Already these forces are at work in today's world and form part of what the apostle Paul calls "the secret power of lawlessness" (or, as the King James Version puts it, "the mystery of iniquity"; see 2 Thessalonians 2:7).

At present there is much good in the world, intermingled with much that is evil. But when the restraints are removed, when the Holy Spirit is taken out of the world, evil will quickly take over all the systems and institutions of human society. We have seen similar events in the past. After the Russian revolution in 1917, godless communism advanced quickly, so that in just a few decades the oppressive doctrine of Marxism-Leninism-Maoism had gained control of most of the Eastern Hemisphere, from Eastern Europe, all across Asia, to the Pacific shores of China. Communism continued to expand into Latin America, Africa, and throughout Asia until it was finally checked in the 1980s and 1990s. It is nothing short of astonishing how quickly the godless communist doctrine wrapped itself around our globe like a boa constrictor, enslaving and murdering millions of human beings.

The collapse of communism in the 1990s should not be confused with the downfall of Russia, which has yet to take place. The story of Russia's destruction is described in the Old Testament book of Ezekiel, in chapters 38 and 39. These passages are supplemented by parallel passages in Daniel 11, Joel 2, and Isaiah 10.

The prophet Ezekiel identifies a great power coming from the north against the land of Israel. He writes:

> The word of the LORD came to me: "Son of man, set your face against Gog, of the land of Magog, the chief prince of Meshech and Tubal; prophesy against him." (Ezekiel 38:1–2)

The land of Magog, also mentioned in Genesis 10, is a general term for an undefined area around the Caspian Sea. The term "chief prince" is even more specific. In Hebrew it is actually "the prince of Rosh." There is much evidence that the name *Russia* is derived from the word *Rosh*. Scholars also identify Meshech and Tubal with the ancient capitals of Russia and Siberia, known today as Moscow and Tobolsk.

Through Ezekiel, God delivers this message to the prince of Rosh:

> After many days you will be called to arms. In future years you will invade a land that has recovered from war, whose people were gathered from many nations to the moun-

tains of Israel, which had long been desolate. They had been brought out from the nations, and now all of them live in safety. You and all your troops and the many nations with you will go up, advancing like a storm; you will be like a cloud covering the land. (Ezekiel 38:8–9)

It would be fascinating to trace the full revelation of Scripture concerning this coming invasion of Israel. We learn from the prophet Joel that Jerusalem will be taken, and Zechariah 14 supplies further details of the onslaught. Daniel adds that the northern army will sweep down into Egypt and North Africa. Having conquered those areas, the commander (Daniel calls him the "king of the north") will hear tidings out of the east and north that trouble him, and he will return to the land of Israel. There on the mountains of Judea, the very same mountains where Jesus and His disciples walked, he will be overwhelmed and destroyed. Ezekiel writes:

"I will execute judgment upon him with plague and bloodshed; I will pour down torrents of rain, hailstones and burning sulfur on him and on his troops and on the many nations with him. And so I will show my greatness and my holiness, and I will make myself known in the sight of many nations. Then they will know that I am the LORD." (Ezekiel 38:22–23)

It is apparent from this description that God Himself will assume the prerogative of dealing with the Russian threat. Whether it will involve nuclear warfare or a purely natural disaster is difficult to determine. At any rate, it is clear that the earth will never be governed from Moscow. The general consensus of biblical scholars would date the destruction of Russia at a point during the first half of Daniel's seventieth week, and before the onset of the Great Tribulation.

Religious Babylon

The one roadblock to power that will remain before the Antichrist can have his way with the world is the towering religious monolith that remains in control of institutional religion after the true church has been removed. The apostle John gave us a symbolic picture of this church in Revelation 17:

> One of the seven angels who had the seven bowls came and said to me, "Come, I will show you the punishment of the great prostitute, who sits on many waters. With her the kings of the earth committed adultery and the inhabitants of the earth were intoxicated with the wine of her adulteries."
>
> Then the angel carried me away in the Spirit into a desert. There I saw a woman sitting on a scarlet beast that was covered with blasphemous names and had seven heads and ten horns. The woman was dressed in purple and scarlet, and was glittering with gold, precious stones and pearls. She held a golden cup in her hand, filled with abominable things and the filth of her adulteries. This title was written on her forehead:
>
> MYSTERY
> BABYLON THE GREAT,
> THE MOTHER OF PROSTITUTES
> AND OF THE ABOMINATIONS OF THE EARTH.
>
> I saw that the woman was drunk with the blood of the saints, the blood of those who bore testimony to Jesus. When I saw her, I was greatly astonished. (Revelation 17:1–6)

The ten-horned beast on which the woman rides is a symbolic description of the Antichrist, who is the head of the political hierarchy of the western world. The woman represents the false church. The beast she rides exercises control over the Antichrist.

The name of this woman is "Mystery Babylon the Great." This strange name indicates that false Christianity is in some way linked with the ancient city of Babylon, located about sixty miles south of Baghdad in modern Iraq. Since Babylon is the city that grew up around the tower of Babel, as described in Genesis 11, we have in that story a strong hint of what the error of Babylonianism is. The tower of Babel was the earliest attempt of man to gain power and prestige by the exercise of religious authority. In that great city by the Euphrates, a false religion arose and masqueraded as the true religion.

Throughout history, false belief has been infiltrating all religious systems to deceive and delude men and women. The characteristics of false belief have always been the same: love of power and prestige, obtained by exercising religious authority.

Babylonianism is not confined to any one church or religious institution. Like the true church, the false church is scattered throughout human society and across the globe, permeating everything. The difference between the true church and the false is the difference between an *organism* and an *organization*. The true church is an organism, a living body, made up of members who share the life of Jesus. The false church is an organization, and stresses political power structures, hierarchies, and institutional membership.

Wherever you find people who bow to the lordship of Jesus Christ, wherever you find people who truly love and obey Him, you find the true church. Wherever you find those who are outwardly religious but love to acquire status, prestige, acclaim, and power, you find the false church, Babylon the Great.

We can see all around us that ecclesiastical merger is the spirit of the day. Almost monthly we read of some new merger of churches or religious organizations. Churches and organizations may blend and merge, but in God's sight, authentic believers and false believers are as different and easily distinguished as black chess pieces are from white. From a human perspective, however, it is impossible to separate the true church from the false until God Himself removes the true and leaves the false behind.

Many Christians ask, "What shall we do about this growing octopus of churches? Should we withdraw and form our own separate, purified group, where unbelief is excluded and only true Christians are admitted?" That is not practical. It is not even possible. Jesus said that the wheat and the weeds should be allowed to grow together until the harvest.

All around us we see various bodies attempting to bring all faiths together in a kind of united super-faith. Thus, we see "ecumenical" this and "interfaith" that. In all likelihood, these groups have genuine Christians on their membership rolls. There are also "pure" and "orthodox" and "evangelical" bodies that have members who are Babylonians at heart. No individual or collection of individuals possesses the wisdom to distinguish between the true and the false. Until God divides the wheat from the weeds in the last day, each individual must judge his or her own heart and make sure that it is a heart of genuine faith.

This may be a harder task than you realize.

The Marks of Counterfeit Christianity

Tragically, many people who believe they are genuine Christians are, in fact, false Christians. How can you know which side you are on?

The Bible indicates that there are certain attitudes that mark a false Christian. Let's take a look at three incisive passages that unveil counterfeit Christianity. The first passage is from Paul's letter to the Philippians:

For, as I have often told you before and now say again even with tears, many live as enemies of the cross of Christ. Their destiny is destruction, their god is their stomach, and their glory is in their shame. Their mind is on earthly things. (Philippians 3:18–19)

One clear mark of false Christianity is a set of wrong values. The most important question any person must ask himself is, "Who or what is my god?" Paul discusses the person whose god is his stomach. These people are not concerned about the work of the Lord, the preaching of the good news of Christ, or the ministry of meeting human need. The real concerns of these people are, "What shall I eat? What shall I drink? How will I be clothed? What will my standard of living be?" They glory in what should be their shame. They boast of their pride, their pettiness, their striving for pleasure and status. They should be ashamed of such things.

Their minds are on "earthly things." They have no vision of the unseen but very real world of heavenly things. Earthly things are not wrong—but they should not be our goal. The ultimate decisions of life should not be based on acquiring wealth and possessions, attaining status, or gaining the praise of people. Our eyes should be set on the absolute values that God declares.

Jesus said, "But seek first his kingdom and his righteousness, and all these things will be given to you as well" (Matthew 6:33). Those who mind earthly things quickly forget the Lord's words when material values are at stake.

The second passage that marks a counterfeit Christian is the sobering statement of the Lord Jesus that is recorded in Matthew's gospel:

"Not everyone who says to me, 'Lord, Lord,' will enter the kingdom of heaven, but only he who does the will of my

Father who is in heaven. Many will say to me on that day, 'Lord, Lord, did we not prophesy in your name, and in your name drive out demons and perform many miracles?' Then I will tell them plainly, 'I never knew you. Away from me, you evildoers!'" (Matthew 7:21–23)

These people are characterized by a false sense of ministry. They are certain that what they have done will win a commendation from Christ, but they are terribly mistaken. They have done many worthy acts: teaching, healing, and helping. "Did we not prophesy in your name?" That is the ministry of teaching and it is apparently Christian teaching, for it is done in the name of Christ. "Did we not cast out demons?" That is the ministry of healing, of counseling and delivering from oppressive powers. "Did we not do many mighty works?" This could include such works as establishing schools, building hospitals, lifting literary standards, and many other activities that the world would recognize as "mighty works."

But there is one thing wrong. All of these works are done for the sake of the self. They are nothing more than an attempt to gain worldly prestige and popular favor by doing religious deeds. It is the essence of Babylonianism. There has been no new beginning, no new birth in Jesus Christ.

The third passage that marks a counterfeit Christian is the statement of Jesus found in the book of Revelation:

"I know your deeds, that you are neither cold nor hot. I wish you were either one or the other! So, because you are lukewarm—neither hot nor cold—I am about to spit you out of my mouth. You say, 'I am rich; I have acquired wealth and do not need a thing.' But you do not realize that you are wretched, pitiful, poor, blind and naked." (Revelation 3:15–17)

These false Christians suffer from a false sense of power. They think they are Christians and call themselves Christians. They even see themselves as an especially rich and powerful church. "Money talks," they say. "Money is power." But money cannot change hearts, or break evil habits, or open deceived eyes. The world reckons success, power, and influence on the basis of big bank accounts, but God is not impressed by wealth. From His point of view, the biggest megachurch with the largest ministry budget could be the most impoverished church in town.

Understand, there is nothing intrinsically wrong with a large church having a lot of money with which to do ministry. There are many faithful, truly Christian churches that are extremely wealthy. But we should be careful never to mistake worldly wealth and influence for godliness.

Moreover, those of us who are members or leaders of large, prosperous churches should beware of the peril of self-confidence. Jesus warns us against the attitude that says, "I am rich; I have acquired wealth and do not need a thing." That is the spirit of Babylonianism. Those who have such an attitude may be outwardly successful, but from God's perspective, they are wretched, blind, and naked.

The Fate of the False Church

The ultimate fate of the false religious system is revealed to us by John in Revelation 17:15–17:

> Then the angel said to me, "The waters you saw, where the prostitute sits, are peoples, multitudes, nations and languages. The beast and the ten horns you saw will hate the

prostitute. They will bring her to ruin and leave her naked; they will eat her flesh and burn her with fire. For God has put it into their hearts to accomplish his purpose by agreeing to give the beast their power to rule, until God's words are fulfilled."

Shorn of its real power by the removal of the true Christians, the whole ecclesiastical structure becomes a hollow mockery. Though it still attempts to ride the beast and wield the same control and political influence it has always exercised, this is no longer possible. Morality without faith is empty and vain. It cannot survive as an empty shell, devoid of God's power and moral authority. When it becomes impossible to conceal the hypocrisy and emptiness of the false church, the nations will turn on it like wild pigs and destroy it.

We see a historical foreview of this event in the days of the French Revolution. During the eighteenth century, there was a widespread revolt in France against corrupt institutional religion. Cathedrals were torn down or turned into marketplaces. Altars were violated. Prostitutes were mockingly invested as priests. Religious teachings were held up to scorn.

In the last days, the nations will hate the harlot that is the false institutional church. They will make her desolate and naked, devouring her flesh and burning her with fire. Then the Antichrist will be unopposed—free to carry out his cruel intentions upon all the peoples of earth.

If, in searching your own heart, you find continual manifestation of self-centeredness, of concern for yourself and lack of concern for others, of bitterness or resentment, then you should know that these are marks of the path of unbelief. Though you may have received the Lord Jesus into your heart, you are not yet living the life He came to give you.

I urge you to ask our Lord to deal with the pride and love of position within you. Ask Him to kindle a flame in your heart—a flame of Christian love and grace. If life is dull and meaningless for you, uncertain and filled with darkness, then somewhere you've failed to take what He came to give.

He did not come to give you darkness, dullness, and drabness. He came to give you life—abundant life, the kind of life He Himself lived when He walked the roads and hillsides of Palestine. If He has entered your heart, then expect Him to live that kind of life in you, for that is what the Christian life is: All of Him, living out all that He is through you!

True Christianity is nothing less than this. ◇

7

The Secret Presence

Matthew 24:23–28

What was the first question ever asked in the New Testament? It was the question asked by wise men who came to Jerusalem from the east: "Where is the one who has been born king of the Jews?" (Matthew 2:2).

When King Herod heard that the wise men had come asking about the birth of the Messiah, he posed the same question to the chief priests and teachers of the law: "Where is the Christ, the Messiah, to be born?"

They told him, "In Bethlehem of Judea."

So the New Testament opens with a search for Christ. It opens with the all-important question, "Where is He?"

Now Jesus stands on the Mount of Olives, giving His followers a preview of that profoundly troubled period of history, the end of the age. And Jesus tells these men that a time is coming when people will ask, "Where is the Christ? Where is the Messiah?" But, He says, that will be a "trick question"—be careful of it! He says:

> "At that time if anyone says to you, 'Look, here is the Christ!' or, 'There he is!' do not believe it. For false Christs and false prophets will appear and perform great signs and

miracles to deceive even the elect—if that were possible. See, I have told you ahead of time.

"So if anyone tells you, 'There he is, out in the desert,' do not go out; or, 'Here he is, in the inner rooms,' do not believe it. For as lightning that comes from the east is visible even in the west, so will be the coming of the Son of Man. Wherever there is a carcass, there the vultures will gather." (Matthew 24:23–28)

Do not miss the words with which Jesus opens this section: "At that time . . . ." This phrase clearly refers to the time of the Great Tribulation He has briefly but ominously described. He says, "If those days had not been cut short, no one would survive, but for the sake of the elect those days will be shortened" (Matthew 24:22). As we have seen, this is the last three-and-a-half years of Daniel's predicted seventieth week.

During this terrible time of persecution and judgment, the Lord Jesus will support and sustain His own people by appearing to them frequently in a variety of places. These appearances will certainly be made to the 144,000 Jewish Christians in their worldwide ministry, and perhaps also to that "great multitude" of Gentile believers who will come out of the Great Tribulation.

As a result of these appearances, rumors will apparently spread like wildfire that the Messiah, the Christ, is somewhere around. Jesus had already predicted that a situation like this would occur during the forty-day period after His resurrection:

Now at the Feast the Jews were watching for him and asking, "Where is that man?" . . .
The Pharisees heard the crowd whispering such things about him.

Then the chief priests and the Pharisees sent temple guards to arrest him. Jesus said, "I am with you for only a short time, and then I go to the one who sent me. You will look for me, but you will not find me; and where I am, you cannot come."

The Jews said to one another, "Where does this man intend to go that we cannot find him? Will he go where our people live scattered among the Greeks, and teach the Greeks? What did he mean when he said, 'You will look for me, but you will not find me,' and 'Where I am, you cannot come'?" (John 7:11, 32–36)

To those Jewish leaders, Jesus was nothing but a tub-thumping, rabble-rousing, troublemaker from Nazareth. They wanted to put Him to death as quickly as possible. Jesus knew their plans—and He knew that their plans would succeed. But He baffled them by saying that after they had done their worst, after they had killed Him, they would look for Him and not be able to find Him. That could have been true only during His forty-day post-resurrection ministry.

After Jesus ascended into the heavens, the Jewish leaders did not look for Him because the disciples were then declaring throughout Jerusalem that He had gone to the Father. But during that forty-day period between the Resurrection and the Ascension, there must have been many disquieting rumors. These rumors, which said that Jesus had been seen here, that He had been seen there, must have been maddening to the Jewish authorities. They thought they had destroyed Him—and now there were reports of His appearing all around! But if they went to look for Him, if they tried to track that rumor to its source, they invariably found that they were too late. Just as Jesus had predicted, they searched for Him but could not find Him.

Jesus appeared to His own—but He completely eluded the Jewish religious leaders. He had established a new and exciting relationship with His faithful followers, and the religious leaders could not intrude on that relationship. They couldn't even understand it.

Pre-Church Christians, Church Christians, and Post-Church Christians

During the forty-day period before Jesus ascended, His disciples had not yet become the church. They were what we might call "pre-church Christians." They believed in Jesus, but the church was not formed until the day of Pentecost when the Holy Spirit was poured out.

During the age in which we now live, the Holy Spirit is among us. The church of Jesus Christ is alive and well and active in the world. We live in what is often called "the Church Age," and we are "church Christians."

At the end of the age, after the church has been removed from the world, there will be new Christian converts. Jesus calls them "the elect." They will be Christians of a new kind—what we might call "post-church Christians." At that point in history, the church will have been removed from the world, and Christians will not be able to have any visible participation in world affairs.

We, the Christians who have been removed from the world (either through death or as a result of the Lord's return for us), will be given glorified bodies like the Lord's. The apostle Paul has said that, once removed from this life, the church will be forever "with the Lord" (1 Thessalonians 4:17). It seems likely that we Christians of the Church Age will join the Lord Jesus in His ministry behind the scenes during the Tribulation. The church Christians will be like Moses and Elijah, who appeared with the transfigured Christ on the Mount (see Mark 9:2–9).

Here is the picture Scripture sketches for us of that time: Jesus will come for His church and take His followers into a new relationship with Him. Then He, along with them, will remain throughout the "end of the age" period, appearing only to those whose hearts are ready to believe in Him. Rumors of His presence will be flying everywhere, and people will say (just as they said during the forty days after His resurrection), "Where is He?" People will search for Him and not be able to find Him. But false prophets will claim to know where He is.

Masters of Deceit

Part of the Tribulation of the end times will be a fresh and powerful campaign of deceit directed against any who are tempted to believe in Jesus. Just as the Lord foresaw the great forces of deception as the end of the age approached, He also foresaw the coordinated campaign of deception during the Great Tribulation.

The first element of this campaign of deception is the rise of powerful, persuasive religious personalities. "For false Christs and false prophets will appear," He says, "and perform great signs and miracles to deceive even the elect—if that were possible" (Matthew 24:24). No program of deception and lying propaganda ever succeeded without a masterful, persuasive leader.

People readily follow those who speak with authority and who manifest powerful, appealing personalities. There is no road to error quite as compelling as a religious one. History shows that more people are misled religiously than in any other way. Almost every false religious movement has had a charming, persuasive, compelling personality in the leadership position. Islam had Muhammad, the Mormon Church had Joseph Smith, the Scientologists had L. Ron Hubbard, the People's Temple had Jim Jones, and on and on.

Lies are much more believable when they are cloaked in religious garb and persuasively presented by a dynamic orator. No one would pay much attention if a blatant atheist were to attack Christian truth. But let a religious leader make the same statements in soothing, religious-sounding tones, and people will swallow the lie as readily as the truth.

So false Christs shall arise, taking full advantage of the superstitious expectancy of the times. As Jesus said in another place, "Men will faint from terror, apprehensive of what is coming on the world" (Luke 21:26). False christs will come with a display of signs and wonders, misleading many, and playing into the hand of the lawless one, the Antichrist.

Not only will there be false christs but also false prophets. We have already seen that there are secular as well as religious prophets. A "prophet," in this sense, is an opinion-leader—perhaps a philosopher, university professor, author, journalist, political leader, or scientist. In secular society, "prophets" are people of great intelligence and influence. When they speak, people listen.

While the church is on earth, it acts as salt, pervading every aspect of society. Godly prophets serve to spread the savor and preservative of salt throughout the world. But at the end of the age, there will no longer be room in secular society for the light of the Christian gospel, no place among intellectuals for what Paul calls "God's secret wisdom, a wisdom that has been hidden" (1 Corinthians 2:7). Since people of faith will no longer have a place among the world's elite, individuals possessing tremendous intellectual ability will arise, becoming instruments of error. These are the false prophets. They will convince millions that the lie of the Antichrist is the essence of reason. They will lead millions to an eternal doom.

The masterful, persuasive personalities of the last days will use the most powerful propaganda techniques ever devised. They will claim to know who and where the Christ is, and they will deceive many. Does it seem unbelievable to you that millions of people could be so deceived by so great a lie? Then let me share a personal experience.

I was once invited to meet a certain Bible "teacher" in a private home. As we sat down to talk, he said to me, "Christ has already returned to earth and I belong to a group of people who know where He is. If you are really interested in preaching the truth, I can tell you how to get in on the secret."

I would have thought his comments laughable if they were not so tragic. Wanting to know just how deluded this man was, I said, "Since you know where Christ is, would you tell me?"

"Oh, He is in a special place in the desert, here in California," the man answered. "I have seen Him and talked with Him many times. Only those who are in the inner circle are permitted to know where He is."

I opened my Bible, turned to Matthew 24:26, and read these words to him: "So if anyone tells you, 'There he is, out in the desert,' do not go out; or, 'Here he is, in the inner rooms,' do not believe it." I thought it significant that this man specifically told me that the Christ was out in the California desert—and Jesus had specifically said, "Don't go out in the desert looking for the Christ!"

But this man was completely unfazed by the clear teaching of Jesus. "Oh," he said, "Jesus wasn't referring to our group when He said that. He was referring to *false* teachers talking about a *false* Christ. But the Christ I'm telling you about is the *true* Christ!"

Well, that is a crackpot approach to prophecy. But many people are perfectly willing to follow crackpots! False followers will readily swallow a false gospel in the last days.

Lightning in the East

As a clincher, Jesus says that these false leaders will "appear and perform great signs and miracles to deceive even the elect—if that were possible" (Matthew 24:24). What form will these signs and miracles take? We do not know. But we see many individuals and movements already in our society who claim to present the truth, attested by signs and miracles.

Some of these false prophets, false christs, and false movements are pseudo-Christian. They maintain the trappings of Christian faith while subtly undermining and distorting biblical truth. Some are New Age cults that teach the deification of the self, and the miraculous power of crystals and herbal magic. Some are covens of witchcraft or Wicca. Others are openly practicing satanists. Some preach that reality is made up of many dimensions or spiritual realms, from which UFOs, alien beings, crop circles, and other manifestations come. There are many -isms and -ologies, and they all claim to be backed by miraculous signs and wonders. Jesus says that some of these signs and wonders will appear so convincing, so miraculous, that even Christians may be fooled by them.

In contrast to the false propaganda and false signs of the last days, Jesus discloses to us a true and foolproof method for finding Him. He says:

"For as lightning that comes from the east is visible even in the west, so will be the coming of the Son of Man. Wher-

ever there is a carcass, there the vultures will gather."
(Matthew 24:27–28)

Here again, as He did in Matthew 24:3, the Lord uses the
word *parousia* to predict His coming. It is a different word than He
uses later when He speaks of "the Son of Man . . . coming on the
clouds of the sky, with power and great glory" (verse 30). It is easy
to confuse these two comings because of His reference to lightning
in verse 27. Since lightning is a form of power and glory, many feel
the Lord is using it as a symbol of His coming in glory. But note
carefully what He says.

When lightning flashes in the east, its effect is seen all over the
sky. Jesus uses the symbol of lightning to describe a manifestation
of glory that takes place in one place but is universally visible. Its
effect is everywhere. Like a flash of lightning, Jesus will be seen by
His own in specific places, at specific times, but the effect of His
various appearances will be felt throughout the earth. Though the
parousia itself will only be witnessed by the Lord's own people, the
effects of the *parousia* will be seen everywhere.

As lightning is unpredictable and uncontrollable, so will be the
presence, the *parousia*, of the Son of Man. He will appear and disappear at will. Whenever there is need for Him, He will be present, just
as He was during the post-resurrection period. There will be no need
to search for Him for He cannot be found that way. There will be no
need to look for Him in the desert or in the inner rooms. He will
come whenever and wherever He finds a heart ready to know Him.

In the parallel passage in Luke, Jesus says, "For the Son of Man
in his day will be like the lightning, which flashes and lights up the
sky from one end to the other" (Luke 17:24). A "day" used in that
sense always refers to a period of time, not a sudden, climactic event.

Using a common proverb of His time, Jesus indicates the proper way to find Him: "Wherever there is a carcass, there the vultures will gather" (Matthew 24:28).

Once, when I was a boy attending a remote high school in Montana, we had an evening basketball practice. At the close of the practice, the coach called one of the team members aside. I watched him go to the other side of the room. The boy was a close friend of mine and came from a poor family, trying to eke out a living on a ranch about ten miles north of town. I watched the boy's face as the coach talked to him. He paled, then walked off with his head lowered.

Then the coach came over to us and said, "I just gave Joe some bad news. His dad has been found dead." Then he told us how he was found.

One of the neighbors owned a ranch about four or five miles away, across a deep canyon from Joe's home. The man had looked over and noticed that there was no smoke rising from the ranch house, so he saddled a horse and rode over. When he came to the cabin, everything was still and no one was around. The rancher wondered if anything was wrong.

Looking to the sky, he saw a group of buzzards circling in the sky about half a mile away. He rode off to investigate and found the body of Joe's father under the circling buzzards. I have never forgotten that incident. I recall that tragedy whenever I read these words of Jesus: "Wherever there is a carcass, there the vultures will gather."

Unmistakable Marks

What does the Lord mean by these words? Why does He compare His appearance on earth to a decaying corpse? He is simply taking a common saying of the day to suggest that whenever you are looking for something, be aware of the accompanying signs. We have a similar proverb today, "Where there's smoke, there's fire."

In the last days, people will ask, "Where is Jesus Christ? How do you find Him?" The answer: Look to those places where you see signs of His activity. They are unmistakable. Jesus comes to transform life, to make life anew. He comes to remove delusion and deception, and to lead us into truth and reality. He comes to deliver us from guilt, fear, and hate. Even in those terrible days of unprecedented violence, terror, and death, Jesus will be busy with His everlasting ministry among human souls.

If you want to know where Jesus is, look for the signs of His activity, look for the evidence of transformed lives. That has always been true. It was true during His ministry two thousand years ago. It is true now of His ministry through His followers on earth. It will be true even in the last days.

Whenever you see evidence of healed, transformed lives, you know Jesus is there. Like lightning, He is sovereign, uncontrollable, unlimited by geography. False faiths and false prophets will claim, "Christ is here! We have Him hidden away in the desert! If you want to find Him, you must come to us!"

But no individual or group of individuals has the corner on Christ. To those of honest faith, He is universally available. He is instantly present with any humble heart that seeks Him. ◇

8

The Power and the Glory

Matthew 24:29–31

Up in the northwest corner of the "boot" of Italy, on the Italian Riviera, is the seaside town of Portofino. Famed for its lush terraced landscape and pastel-painted Old World buildings, this beautiful resort town was once a small fishing village. Here, shellfishers dived for mussels and clams in the bay of San Fruttuoso and deep-sea fishing boats sailed toward the blue waters of the Mediterranean Sea.

If you know where to look, you can find a nine-foot-tall bronze statue of Jesus Christ. That statue is one of the most famous landmarks associated with the town of Portofino. Thousands of tourists and vacationers stream through Portofino every year, enjoying its warm, sunny climate, elegant villas and hotels, and historic architecture—yet only a comparative handful of people have ever seen that famed statue of Christ.

Why? Because the statue is under fifty feet of water!

The statue is called the Christ of the Abysses, and it is located in the waters of the bay. On an exceptionally calm and sunny day, it can sometimes be glimpsed from a boat on the surface. But throughout most of the year, it can be seen only by divers, many of whom consider it their protector.

The Christ of the Abysses is hard to find and rarely glimpsed. But a day is coming when Jesus Himself will appear, and everyone in the world will see Him. It will be impossible not to see Him. That day will be the most dramatic event in human history—the day of the visible appearing of Jesus Christ. It is an event that Jesus Himself describes for us in His Olivet prophecy:

> "Immediately after the distress of those days
> 'the sun will be darkened,
>   and the moon will not give its light;
> the stars will fall from the sky,
>   and the heavenly bodies will be shaken.'

> "At that time the sign of the Son of Man will appear in the sky, and all the nations of the earth will mourn. They will see the Son of Man coming on the clouds of the sky, with power and great glory. And he will send his angels with a loud trumpet call, and they will gather his elect from the four winds, from one end of the heavens to the other." (Matthew 24:29–31)

This is the most prophesied event in the Bible. The Old Testament contains many references to it. Some Bible scholars estimate that one-tenth of all the verses in the New Testament refer to this event, the coming of Jesus Christ at the close of history. If all the references to Christ's return were removed, the New Testament would become virtually unintelligible. So the event we are about to examine is clearly one of the most important occurrences in all of history.

The Splendor of His Coming

Many Christians confuse the presence (or *parousia*) of Jesus with the sudden, worldwide, visible appearance of Jesus. The *parousia* begins when the church is taken out of the world. It is commonly called the "rapture" of the church. In that event, which takes place before the end of the age begins, the church is removed from the restrictions of time and Jesus becomes secretly present in the world. Jesus is secretly seen by His own during the dark days of the Tribulation, but the world does not see Him.

Then comes a moment that marks the end of His secret presence—the brilliant, globally visible event of His appearance when Jesus ends the secrecy of His presence and the whole world suddenly sees Him. This is the outshining of His presence before a thunderstruck world, the dramatic unveiling of the One who has already been secretly on earth among His people.

At that moment, Jesus will confront the lawless one, the man of lawlessness, the Antichrist. Paul writes of that moment, saying, "And then the lawless one will be revealed, whom the Lord Jesus will overthrow with the breath of his mouth and destroy by the splendor of his coming" (2 Thessalonians 2:8).

That last phrase, "the splendor of his coming," is literally "the *epiphany* of His *parousia.*" *Epiphany* means "unveiling" or "outshining." So, in other words, Paul calls this dramatic appearance of Jesus Christ "the unveiling of his presence." It is the startling climax of the whole period that Jesus calls "the close of the age."

Humanity's final hour is described for us as a series of three astonishing occurrences of escalating power and importance. The first of these three events involves catastrophe and destruction in the natural realm:

> "Immediately after the distress of those days
> 'the sun will be darkened,
>   and the moon will not give its light;
> the stars will fall from the sky,
>   and the heavenly bodies will be shaken.'" (Matthew 24:29)

Notice that the Lord Jesus makes a clear distinction between this event and the preceding time called the Great Tribulation. The Tribulation is a time when the naked brutality of human beings is widely manifested, when there is unbelievable cruelty and violence throughout society—which is what happens when humanity is completely unrestrained by the grace of God. The Tribulation is described for us in detail in the book of the Revelation, especially in the judgments of the seals and the trumpets. It will be a time when the horrors of Nazi persecution, the gas chambers of Buchenwald and Dachau, will be repeated a hundred times over throughout the earth; a time when violence stalks those in the streets, and nuclear terror rains down from the skies. It will be a time, as Jesus said, of unprecedented evil, slaughter, and human misery.

But immediately following the Tribulation is a natural catastrophe of unimaginable scale. Terrifying signs will appear in the heavens. Note especially the phrase, "and the heavenly bodies will be shaken." This suggests a severe gravitational disturbance in our solar system. A disruption on that scale would produce phenomenal effects on the earth, ranging from frightening displays of falling meteors in our skies to deadly, destructive earthquakes and tidal waves. Volcanoes will erupt, spouting lava and toxic clouds of cinder and ash, darkening the sun while reddening and obscuring the moon. In Luke's parallel account of the Olivet discourse, Jesus says:

> "There will be signs in the sun, moon and stars. On the earth, nations will be in anguish and perplexity at the roaring and tossing of the sea. Men will faint from terror, apprehensive of what is coming on the world, for the heavenly bodies will be shaken. At that time they will see the Son of Man coming in a cloud with power and great glory." (Luke 21:25–27)

In that great and terrible day, all the people of the world will instantly know whether they have made the right or wrong choice with their lives. It will be, for some, a moment of infinite joy; for others, it will be a moment of infinite terror and horror. As C. S. Lewis observed in *Mere Christianity*, "I wonder whether people who ask God to interfere openly and directly in our world quite realize what it will be like when He does. When that happens, it is the end of the world. When the author walks onto the stage, the play is over. . . . It will be too late then to choose your side. There is no use saying you choose to lie down when it has become impossible to stand up. That will not be the time for choosing. It will be the time when we discover which side we really have chosen."

Voices from the Past

Jesus is not the only person to describe the catastrophic events coming at the end of the age. Old Testament prophets have also foretold these disasters. Compare the prophecy of Jesus with the words of the prophet Joel:

> I will show wonders in the heavens and on the earth,
>   blood and fire and billows of smoke.
> The sun will be turned to darkness and the moon to
>   blood
>   before the coming of the great and dreadful day
>   of the LORD. (Joel 2:30–31)

The Old Testament prophet Isaiah described the same event in strikingly similar language:

> See, the day of the LORD is coming—
>   a cruel day, with wrath and fierce anger—

> to make the land desolate
>> and destroy the sinners within it.
> The stars of heaven and their constellations
>> will not show their light.
> The rising sun will be darkened
>> and the moon will not give its light.
>
> (Isaiah 13:9–10)

In the New Testament, the apostle John described a vision of that same cataclysm. In the book of Revelation, he wrote:

> I watched as he opened the sixth seal. There was a great earthquake. The sun turned black like sackcloth made of goat hair, the whole moon turned blood red, and the stars in the sky fell to earth, as late figs drop from a fig tree when shaken by a strong wind. The sky receded like a scroll, rolling up, and every mountain and island was removed from its place.
>
> (Revelation 6:12–14)

All these passages confirm the dire prophecy of Jesus: A day will come when some cataclysmic celestial force will create tremendous, terrifying events upon earth. These catastrophes will signal the swift-approaching end of the long and bloody history of human civilization.

The Unveiling of Christ

We have just seen the first in a series of three escalating occurrences that mark for us humanity's final hour: A violent natural catastrophe in the heavens and upon the earth. This violent upheaval in nature is followed immediately by the second astonishing occurrence: The sign of the Son of Man in the heavens. Jesus says,

> "At that time the sign of the Son of Man will appear in the
> sky, and all the nations of the earth will mourn." (Matthew
> 24:30)

That word "sign" is important. The second event that marks humanity's final hour is the appearance of a sign in the sky—the sign of the Son of Man. Remember that the Olivet discourse was the result of a question that the disciples of Jesus asked Him. In Matthew 24:3, they said, "What will be the sign of your coming and of the end of the age?" Now, in verse 30, Jesus answers their question—though the answer He gives is not as clear and understandable as the disciples might have liked, or, for that matter, as we would like.

When the disciples asked that question, they did not mean (as we frequently take it), "What is the sign that will mark the time of your coming?" We tend to associate "signs" with schedules. But that is not what the disciples were thinking of. They were asking Jesus, "What is the event that will reveal the *meaning* of your coming?" This is always the purpose of signs in Scripture. That sign, Jesus now says, will appear in the sky just before He is made visible.

It is crucial to note that Jesus links this sign with the statement, "and all the nations of the earth will mourn." That is the New International Version's translation of that statement. The King James Version and the 1901 American Standard Version both translate this statement, "and then shall all the tribes of the earth mourn." The Greek word that is here translated "nations" or "tribes" is *phule*. It is most commonly used in the New Testament to refer to a tribe or kindred group—and especially to one of the twelve tribes of Israel. The Greek word commonly used to refer to nations (particularly Gentile nations, "the nations of the earth") is *ethnos*. But that is not the word used here.

When Jesus says "all the tribes of the earth will mourn," the Greek word for earth is *ge*. In the Greek New Testament, *ge* usually refers to the soil, the ground, or a tract of land within fixed boundaries, such as the nation of Israel. It is less common in the New Testament for *ge* to refer to the entire world.

So I believe the NIV is less accurate here than the KJV and the ASV. Jesus is saying that when the sign of the Son of Man appears in the sky all the tribes of the land of Israel will mourn. If the sign of the Son of Man is linked with Israel, then the evidence strongly suggests that the sign will consist of the reappearance of the cloud of glory that accompanied the nation Israel in the days of Moses. That cloud of glory was called the Shekinah. It was the sign of God's presence with His people, Israel, while they wandered in the wilderness for forty years.

Many years later, when the temple was built and Solomon dedicated it to God, the Shekinah glory came down and took residence above the ark of the covenant in the Holy of Holies in the temple. The Shekinah glory was the sign that God dwelt among His people.

This shining cloud of glory may well be what Jesus Himself refers to when He says, "They will see the Son of Man coming on the clouds of the sky, with power and great glory" (Matthew 24:30). There is an obvious reference to this same event in the book of Revelation. There John says:

> Look, he is coming with the clouds,
>   and every eye will see him,
> even those who pierced him;
>   and all the peoples of the earth will mourn because
>   of him. (Revelation 1:7)

Of course, this passage may simply refer to the atmospheric clouds, but the repeated emphasis seems suggestive of more. When

Jesus appears, it will mark the close of the age. But His appearance will also signal the opening of a new chapter in God's program. The supreme characteristic of that new chapter will be the profound fact that God dwells with His people. The apostle John relates how this fact was revealed to him in his vision:

> And I heard a loud voice from the throne saying, "Now the dwelling of God is with men, and he will live with them. They will be his people, and God himself will be with them and be their God." (Revelation 21:3)

Since the Shekinah is the sign of God's presence with man, it is fitting that the Shekinah would reappear as the sign that explains, clarifies, and reveals the meaning of Christ's coming. He comes that He may be, as the Old Testament prophets whispered, "Immanuel— God with us."

In Power and Great Glory

We have just seen the second of three escalating occurrences that mark humanity's final hour: The sign of the Son of Man in the heavens, the shining cloud of the Shekinah glory. The shining cloud will be followed by the dramatic appearance of Jesus Christ Himself. It is not a silent appearing, not something that takes place in a corner, but a bold, triumphant revelation.

The dramatic appearance of Jesus is often called the "Second Coming of Christ," though to be precise, the term *Second Coming* actually refers to the entire period of Christ's secret presence as well as His appearance to the world. This dramatic unveiling is, in fact, the second time the world sees Jesus Christ. The last time the world saw Him, He was hanging on a blood-stained cross, writhing in His death-agony. He looked like a complete failure—without power, without honor, without glory. But the next time the world sees Him, He will appear in power and triumph. All glory will belong to Him.

As John declared in Revelation 1:7, "every eye will see him." And as Paul wrote to the Thessalonians:

> God is just: He will pay back trouble to those who trouble you and give relief to you who are troubled, and to us as well. This will happen when the Lord Jesus is revealed from heaven in blazing fire with his powerful angels. He will punish those who do not know God and do not obey the gospel of our Lord Jesus. (2 Thessalonians 1:6–8)

The present age, when God allows human beings to exercise their rebellious will upon the planet, is finally brought to an end. God now reasserts His right to rule over all the earth. This moment is described with striking language and imagery in the book of Revelation:

> The seventh angel sounded his trumpet, and there were loud voices in heaven, which said:
>
> "The kingdom of the world has become the kingdom of
>   our Lord and of his Christ,
>   and he will reign for ever and ever." (Revelation 11:15)

When Jesus says in the Olivet discourse that the whole world "will see the Son of Man coming on the clouds of the sky, with power and great glory," we are reminded of the closing words of the Lord's Prayer: "For thine is the kingdom and the power, and the glory, forever. Amen" (Matthew 6:13, NASB). The prayer that our Lord taught His disciples to pray reflects the anticipation of God's people, through all the dark centuries, of the approaching day when the power and the glory of the universe will be in the hands of the One to whom it rightfully belongs. That is our hope and our confidence as Christians.

Satan, of course, does not want Jesus to have the power and the glory. Three times, Satan tempted Jesus in the wilderness in order to prevent Jesus from attaining the power and the glory that was rightfully His. In the third and final temptation, Satan took Jesus to a high mountain and showed Him all the kingdoms of the world in a moment of time. There Satan said to Him, "All this I will give you if you will bow down and worship me." In effect, Satan was saying, "The kingdom, the power, and the glory are *mine*, not yours." And Satan was right—for the moment.

Jesus did not rebuke Satan for making a preposterous claim that had no justification. Instead, He answered Satan using the only weapon available to a believer in an hour of darkness or temptation: the unchangeable word of God. Jesus said to him: "Away from me, Satan! For it is written: 'Worship the Lord your God, and serve him only'" (Matthew 4:10).

With those words, Jesus set aside the temptation to take a short-cut to power and glory. Jesus had come in order to receive the power and glory that was His—but the way to that power and glory led through the cross. Satan offered an easy path to glory. Jesus chose, instead, the hard path, the narrow way, the darkness, agony, and humiliation of the cross. But in doing so, He made possible a future moment—the very moment described here in the Olivet discourse, when He will appear before the entire human race. It is the moment when He will come in power and great glory to take His place over the kingdoms of the world.

When Israel Mourns

The unveiling of Jesus as King of kings and Lord of lords will accomplish certain immediate results. The first will be the mourning of the nation of Israel. As we have already noted, the Lord states in His Olivet discourse that all the tribes of the land of Israel will mourn. And in the book of Revelation, John says, "all the peoples of the earth will mourn because of him" (Revelation 1:7). There will be national sorrow in Israel, as well as global sorrow.

This time of great mourning fulfills the Old Testament prophecy of Zechariah, in which the prophet says:

> "And I will pour out on the house of David and the inhabitants of Jerusalem a spirit of grace and supplication. They will look on me, the one they have pierced, and they will mourn for him as one mourns for an only child, and grieve bitterly for him as one grieves for a firstborn son. On that day the weeping in Jerusalem will be great, like the weeping of Hadad Rimmon in the plain of Megiddo." (Zechariah 12:10–11)

Why will they mourn? Because they will see the One whom they have pierced, and they will realize their sin and error. To their utter astonishment, they will discover that the One who appears in power and great glory bears wounds that they themselves have inflicted. They will see the wounds in His hands, the marks of nails. They will see the wound in His side, the piercing wound of the spear. And they will see the wounds they have inflicted on Him by rejecting Him and spurning the sacrifice He made for them upon the cross.

In a strange and tragic way, it will also be a fulfillment of the demand of the crowd who called for the death of Jesus. In Matthew

27:22–25, we see that the crowd demanded, "Crucify him! . . . Crucify him! . . . Let his blood be on us and on our children!" And so it was. And that is why the world will mourn in grief over the One they have pierced.

Perhaps the very words of their mourning are recorded for us in a well-known passage from the prophet Isaiah. According to that Old Testament prophecy, there will come a day when Israel shall look on Him whom they have pierced, and they will say to each other:

> He was despised and rejected by men,
>   a man of sorrows, and familiar with suffering.
> Like one from whom men hide their faces
>   he was despised, and we esteemed him not.
> Surely he took up our infirmities
>   and carried our sorrows,
> yet we considered him stricken by God,
>   smitten by him, and afflicted.
> But he was pierced for our transgressions,
>   he was crushed for our iniquities;
> the punishment that brought us peace was upon him,
>   and by his wounds we are healed. (Isaiah 53:3–5)

On the day that Jesus is revealed to the world in power and great glory, the people of Israel will recognize that the One whom their fathers crucified in ignorance and blindness was the One who loved them and gave Himself for their sins. They will mourn and weep not only for His pain, His wounds, His suffering on their behalf, but also for their own rejection of the One who gave Himself for them.

Righteousness Triumphs—At Last!

But that is not all that will happen in Israel when Jesus appears in power and glory. Concerning Himself, Jesus adds:

> "And he will send his angels with a loud trumpet call, and they will gather his elect from the four winds, from one end of the heavens to the other." (Matthew 24:31)

Who is Jesus talking about? Who are the "elect"? We do not need to be in doubt about the identity of God's elect. In the Old Testament, the prophet Isaiah tells us:

> In that day the Lord will reach out his hand a second time to reclaim the remnant that is left of his people from Assyria, from Lower Egypt, from Upper Egypt, from Cush, from Elam, from Babylonia, from Hamath and from the islands of the sea.
>
> He will raise a banner for the nations
>   and gather the exiles of Israel;
> he will assemble the scattered people of Judah
>   from the four quarters of the earth.
>
> (Isaiah 11:11–12)

The prophet Jeremiah confirms the same promise. Jeremiah chapter 31, loved by many for the beauty of its language and the gladness of its promise, contains this wonderful prophecy about the elect of God:

> This is what the LORD says:
> "Sing with joy for Jacob;
>   shout for the foremost of the nations.
> Make your praises heard, and say,
>   'O LORD , save your people, the remnant of Israel.'

> See, I will bring them from the land of the north
>   and gather them from the ends of the earth.
> Among them will be the blind and the lame,
>   expectant mothers and women in labor;
>   a great throng will return." (Jeremiah 31:7–8)

The gathering that the Lord promises through the prophet Jeremiah will undoubtedly include the 144,000 Jewish believers who are sealed, according to Revelation 7:4. Perhaps it will include as many as are left alive of the "great multitude" of Gentiles who believe in Jesus because of the testimony of the remnant of Israel. In the parable of the wheat and the weeds, Jesus Himself describes this same gathering of elect believers, and His description suggests that there are Gentiles included as well as Jewish believers:

> "As the weeds are pulled up and burned in the fire, so it will be at the end of the age. The Son of Man will send out his angels, and they will weed out of his kingdom everything that causes sin and all who do evil. They will throw them into the fiery furnace, where there will be weeping and gnashing of teeth. Then the righteous will shine like the sun in the kingdom of their Father. He who has ears, let him hear." (Matthew 13:40–43)

Some Christians believe that this gathering up of the righteous by the angels is the same event as the removal (or Rapture) of the church, as described by Paul in 1 Thessalonians 4. I am convinced, however, that this gathering of the righteous is not the same event. Jesus does not say anything here about gathering the elect into heaven. Rather, His parable suggests that living believers are gathered into an earthly kingdom. In this parable, Jesus does not mention the resurrection of the dead; however, in the case of the removal of the church from the world, resurrection is a primary emphasis.

Also, when the church is removed, as Paul relates in 1 Thessalonians 4, there is no indication that evil men are judged. But in the Lord's parable of the wheat and the weeds in Matthew 13, Jesus makes it very clear that "everything that causes sin and all who do evil" will be removed from His kingdom at the same time that the elect are gathered. He underscores this fact in another parable in the same chapter:

> "Once again, the kingdom of heaven is like a net that was let down into the lake and caught all kinds of fish. When it was full, the fishermen pulled it up on the shore. Then they sat down and collected the good fish in baskets, but threw the bad away. This is how it will be at the end of the age. The angels will come and separate the wicked from the righteous and throw them into the fiery furnace, where there will be weeping and gnashing of teeth." (Matthew 13:47–50)

It is logical to suppose that this is the time that the lawless one, the Antichrist, will come to his well-deserved end, as described by the apostle John from his vision in the book of Revelation:

> Then I saw the beast and the kings of the earth and their armies gathered together to make war against the rider on the horse and his army [the rider, of course, is the Lord Jesus]. But the beast was captured, and with him the false prophet who had performed the miraculous signs on his behalf. With these signs he had deluded those who had received the mark of the beast and worshiped his image. The two of them were thrown alive into the fiery lake of burning sulfur. The rest of them were killed with the sword that came out of the mouth of the rider on the horse, and all the birds gorged themselves on their flesh. (Revelation 19:19–21)

So ends the reign of the Antichrist—and with his destruction, the reign of evil is ended as well. Righteousness has triumphed on the earth at last. The Lord Jesus Christ receives what was rightfully His from the beginning—the power and great glory of the King of kings and Lord of lords.

The Lesson of Israel

In His Olivet preview of His dramatic return to earth, the Lord Jesus has laid great emphasis on how this event will affect the nation of Israel. Non-Jewish readers may ask, "What is the significance of all these events for us?" As we have previously seen, whenever God wants us to understand how He works in the lives of Christian believers, He uses His workings in the life of the nation of Israel as an object lesson.

As we retrace the history of Israel, we see that everything God did in the life of the nation of Israel, He has done in our lives as believers. The people of Israel were slaves, living in bondage in the land of Egypt, just as we were once slaves, living in bondage to sin that ruled our lives. But the angel of death passed over the people of Israel and spared them in that first Passover. At that moment, they were born as a nation by the grace of God—the Israelites were redeemed, brought out of bondage, and set free. As believers, we know that Jesus was sacrificed for us on the cross during Passover. Just as the blood of a lamb was smeared on the doorways of the houses of Israel, the blood of the Lamb of God stained the cross— and that cross became our doorway to freedom and salvation.

Three months after the Lord brought the Israelites out of Egypt, the people camped in the desert at the foot of Mount Sinai. Moses went up on the mountain and talked with God, and God gave him a message to take back to the people: "You yourselves have seen what I did to Egypt, and how I carried you on eagles' wings and brought you to myself" (Exodus 19:4). In the Bible, an eagle is usually a symbol of God's power. We see this symbol, for example, in Isaiah 40:31: "But those who hope in the LORD will renew their strength. They will soar on wings like eagles."

You may recall that J. R. R. Tolkien drew upon this same potent symbol of divine strength in *The Lord of the Rings*. In that book, Gwaihir, the great lord of the eagles of Middle Earth, rescues Gandalf from prison atop the tower of Orthanc, and then rescues the hobbits, Frodo and Sam, from the fiery Mount Doom in the land of Mordor. That is what the redeeming strength of God is like, swooping into our prisons of sin and despair, rescuing us from the clutches of our enemies, redeeming our souls from the fiery pit, lifting us to unimagined heights of peace and joy. That is what God did for the nation of Israel when He carried them out of Egypt on eagles' wings. That is what God has done for every sinner who is saved by His grace.

But Israel repaid the Lord's goodness and grace with pride and self-righteous attempts to please God without hearts of true worship and love. The people of Israel murmured, grumbled, and complained. They fell into moral failure and sin. And that is so often what happens in the life of the believer. We respond to God's redeeming grace with pride, with attempting to please God with our own self-righteousness, with grumbling and ingratitude and sin. Like Israel, we even slip into patterns of unbelief and rebellion.

When we, as Christians, feel that we are wandering aimlessly in a wilderness of hopelessness and despair, we would do well to ask ourselves, "How is my life like the life of Israel? Is my 'wandering in the wilderness' the result of the same kinds of patterns that caused the people of Israel to wander in the wilderness after being redeemed out of Egypt?" For forty years, the nation of Israel wandered in the desert before they came into the Land of Promise.

Forty years after the crucifixion of Jesus, Israel was destroyed as a nation and dispersed as a people. Even so, God preserved Israel. For centuries, the Jewish people have been dispersed throughout the length and breadth of the earth. Though their temple was destroyed and they have largely fallen into disbelief, the people of Israel have been preserved as a nation, as a distinct culture, as a unique people. When the nation of Israel was carved out of the former British protectorate of Palestine in 1948, the Jewish people once again had a homeland. Many returned to Israel and reestablished themselves as a nation—but they did so largely in unbelief.

But, says Jesus, the hour is coming when God will gather the Jewish people from all around the world and bring them back to the land. This will happen by an act of God's own sovereign grace, without any merit on the part of the Jewish people—just as you and I, as Christians, are saved by His sovereign grace, having done nothing to earn our salvation.

The time when Jesus is revealed to Israel and to all the world will be an hour of mourning and repentance. Every eye will see Him, and every ear will understand at last what God has desired to accomplish in their lives. The people of Israel will then enter into a time of national healing and wholeness. Israel will become God's instrument of blessing to all the earth.

If you read the book of Romans with care, you will see that the same story is told in Romans 5 through 8. There, Paul details for us the way God has designed to bring men and women into genuine liberty, genuine joy, and the true excitement of life. In Romans 9 through 11, Israel is brought in as the illustration of these principles. Paul uses Israel as the example of how God will work in our own lives.

When we come to the place of utter spiritual bankruptcy, when we stop thinking we can contribute something of value to God, when we finally begin to rest and rely wholly upon His power to redeem us and work through us—then we begin to enter into the fullness of life that God has planned for us. That is the meaning of God's dealings with Israel. That is the meaning of God's plan for your life and mine. ◇

9

A Thief in the Night

———

Matthew 24:32–44

Girolamo Cardano was one of the greatest mathematicians of the sixteenth century. He was also a great believer in astrology, the "art" of foretelling a person's future on the basis of signs and omens in the planets and stars. Born in Pavia, Italy, in 1501, Cardano cast his own horoscope, then predicted that he would die on September 21, 1576, at the age of seventy-five.

History records that Cardano did indeed die on the exact date predicted!

But on closer inspection, this fact is not as amazing as it might seem. On the appointed day of his death, Cardano arose from his bed and found himself in excellent health. Knowing that he had to die that day or his astrological prediction would be proved false, Cardano committed suicide.

Well, that's *one* way of making sure a prediction comes true!

As you have been surveying the prophecies Jesus made in the Olivet discourse, you have undoubtedly wondered when and how all of these things will come to pass. You may want to know exactly what date God has in mind for the culmination of His plan for human history. You may even have doubts that these prophecies will come to pass.

You are not the first person to ask these questions. While Jesus was unfolding the Olivet prophecy to His disciples, I suspect He saw an inquisitive look on their faces. He read the questions in their eyes: "When, Lord? How will it happen, Lord? How can we know for sure, Lord?" So Jesus breaks away from His description of the last days to address the questions that are on our minds, as I'm sure they were on the minds of His disciples. In this passage, He offers three powerful guarantees that everything He has said will truly come to pass. Here is the first:

> "Now learn this lesson from the fig tree: As soon as its twigs get tender and its leaves come out, you know that summer is near. Even so, when you see all these things, you know that it is near, right at the door." (Matthew 24:32)

The Lord draws a pattern from nature to illustrate the point He wishes to make. Everyone knows that when trees begin to put forth their leaves it is an infallible indication that summer is near. Some have misread this to mean that the fig tree is a symbol for the nation Israel, and that the Lord is telling us that when Israel shows signs of life as a nation, the end is near. That is perfectly true, of course, but that is not what Jesus is saying. In the parallel passage in Luke, Jesus says that this parable is not only a parable of the fig tree, but of "all the trees" (Luke 21:29).

What is the Lord telling us? Simply this: As history unfolds and it becomes apparent that the world is heading toward the conditions Jesus has described in the Olivet discourse, then we can be sure that His coming is near. The trend of world events is the guarantee that He has been telling the truth about the future. History will confirm His predictions because history will unfold in perfect alignment with all that He has said. When the world reaches the stage He describes, and the coming of the Antichrist looms on the horizon of global events, then we know that the arrival of Jesus "is near, right at the door."

Here we stand at the end of two thousand years of Christian history. The land of Israel is revived. In that land, plans are already being drawn to rebuild the temple and restore the Old Testament pattern of Jewish worship. Many of Israel's former friends have begun to switch sides and question the right of Israel to exist. The enemies of Israel are amassing all around the tiny nation, seeking an opportunity to drive the Jewish people into the sea.

Has the "tree" of history begun to put out its "leaves," as Jesus pictures for us in His prophecy? I will let you judge for yourself whether the world is moving closer and closer to the events Jesus foretold in His Olivet prophecy.

The Indestructible Generation

Next, the Lord offers a second guarantee, contained in a statement that is widely misinterpreted and misunderstood:

> "I tell you the truth, this generation will certainly not pass away until all these things have happened." (Matthew 24:34)

Many people have wondered exactly what Jesus meant by those words. Was He referring to the generation to which He was speaking—the disciples and their contemporaries? Many critics of the Christian faith have claimed this to be so. They say, "Jesus predicted that the people He was speaking to on the Mount of Olives would still be alive when the world came to an end. Clearly, that generation died out and the world did not end. So the prophecy of Jesus has been proven null and void."

Others have suggested that Jesus was saying that the generation on earth when these events begin will still be living when they are completed. To accept this interpretation, however, one must accept a forced and unnatural meaning for the word "this" in the phrase "this generation."

As I have studied these words and compared them with other passages of Scripture, I have concluded that neither of these is the correct interpretation. The key to understanding this statement is the phrase "this generation." I believe that Jesus uses the phrase *this generation* as a reference to the Jewish people. He is saying, in effect, "This people, the Jewish people, will not pass away until all these things take place."

At first glance, you may think this is a forced interpretation of Jesus' words. But once you understand both the biblical context and the language and cultural context of this statement, you will see that this is, in fact, the most logical and natural interpretation of these words.

First, the biblical context makes it clear that this is what Jesus means. He used this same word, "generation" (Greek *genea*), in the same sense just one chapter earlier. Speaking sharply to the Pharisees, He said:

> "You snakes! You brood of vipers! How will you escape being condemned to hell? Therefore I am sending you prophets and wise men and teachers. Some of them you will kill and crucify; others you will flog in your synagogues and pursue from town to town. And so upon you will come all the righteous blood that has been shed on earth, from the blood of righteous Abel to the blood of Zechariah son of Berekiah, whom you murdered between the temple and the altar. I tell you the truth, all this will come upon this generation." (Matthew 23:33–36)

That last word "generation" is, again, the Greek word *genea*. By that term, Jesus clearly was not referring only to the first-century Pharisees and their first-century contemporaries. He was not saying that a group of people who lived in one time in history would bear the blame for the injustice of the ages.

No, Jesus meant that the generation known as Israel was chosen to be the instrument of God to teach the whole world what God is like. When Israel failed, the nation itself became the recipient of all the dire results that come from a major moral and spiritual failure.

Look, too, at the language and cultural context of that word "generation." In the first century, the word *genea* referred to a group of people of common family stock, of shared nativity or descent. In this sense, everyone who was descended from Jacob—from his twelve sons to King David to Jesus Christ and beyond—were all of the same "generation," the same *genea*, the same group of people known collectively as Israel. This *genea* covers thousands of years of history, but it is all one "generation" in the sense that Jesus clearly uses it here.

While it is true that *genea* can also refer to a group of people who are living in the same time, or to a space of time covering roughly thirty years, the context makes it clear that Jesus was referring to the nation of Israel. The testimony of history also confirms this interpretation.

Throughout twenty centuries of dispersion and persecution, the Jewish people have given the world a remarkable demonstration of the reliability of God's Word. The Jewish people have been targeted for destruction and genocide several times in their history. In my own lifetime, the world witnessed an unprecedented atrocity: the systematic extermination of six million Jewish people. That death toll constituted one-third of the entire Jewish population in the world, 90 percent of all Jews in eastern Europe, and fully 1.5 million Jewish children. Of the three million Jews living in Poland in 1939, roughly 100,000 remained in 1945. Eighty percent of the world's rabbis, Jewish scholars, Jewish teachers, and Jewish students were slaughtered.

It is difficult for Gentiles—non-Jews—to comprehend the horror of the event we call the Holocaust, and which Jews call the Shoah. But this is certain: It is the one event that dominates the Jewish psyche today. It has scarred and scorched the Jewish soul, damaging the ability of many Jewish people to have any faith in humanity or in God.

Yet the Holocaust has also shown us something profound: the Jewish people are an indestructible race. As a people they have survived centuries of dispersion, persecution, pogroms, and genocidal insanity. Without question, Satan has been obsessed with the destruction of God's special people, yet God's promise to Israel has been proven true again and again through the centuries: "whoever touches you touches the apple of [God's] eye" (Zechariah 2:8). Those nations that have enslaved, attacked, and persecuted the Jewish people have always ended up on the ash-heap of history—yet the Jewish people survive.

What Jesus promised in the Olivet discourse has been proven true down through the centuries: "this generation will certainly not pass away until all these things have happened."

Surer than the Sunrise

What Jesus has predicted will surely come to pass. This is the third assurance Jesus offers: His own infallible promise:

> "Heaven and earth will pass away, but my words will never pass away." (Matthew 24:35)

Do you believe those words? The One who spoke them declared that He would give His life as a ransom for many—and He did. He said He would rise again from the dead—and He did. Now He says He will come again—and the question is: Do you believe Him?

What is the one thing in this world that everyone takes for granted as an unchanging, dependable reality? The sun will always rise tomorrow. We never know if we will live to see the next sunrise, but we know that it will come nonetheless. Sunrise, sunset, day after day, the world keeps spinning in its orbit, one revolution every twenty-four hours. We regulate our lives by that unchanging pattern.

But Jesus has made an amazing statement: He says His own words are more durable than the unchanging pattern of this world. "Heaven and earth will pass away," He says, "but my words will never pass away." The earth will stop spinning in its orbit, the sun will cease rising and setting, before the words of Jesus pass away! What does that tell us? It tells us that the promise of His return is more certain than the most certain thing we know—more certain than the sunrise, more durable than the universe itself, more trustworthy than the laws of nature. Paul tells us that Jesus Himself created the universe: "all things were created by him and for him" (Colossians 1:16). The existence of the entire universe rests on the word of the One who has said, "My words will never pass away."

Unpredictable Timing

At this point we come to a definite break in the Lord's prophetic discourse. Jesus has completed His outline of the events at the end of the age. He has revealed His *parousia*, His presence on earth, during the entire period of the last days. He has pulled back the curtain from the spectacular outshining of His presence on earth when every eye shall see Him. Now Jesus underscores the awesome meaning of that event in individual lives. He says:

> "No one knows about that day or hour, not even the
> angels in heaven, nor the Son, but only the Father. As it was
> in the days of Noah, so it will be at the coming of the Son of
> Man. For in the days before the flood, people were eating and
> drinking, marrying and giving in marriage, up to the day
> Noah entered the ark; and they knew nothing about what
> would happen until the flood came and took them all away.
> That is how it will be at the coming of the Son of Man. Two
> men will be in the field; one will be taken and the other left.
> Two women will be grinding with a hand mill; one will be
> taken and the other left." (Matthew 24:36–41)

At this point you may be confused: Which "coming" is Jesus talking about here? Is He talking about His arrival to remove the church from the world—the event that is often called the Rapture? Or is He talking about His glorious manifestation to the world as described in Matthew 24:30? Many people confuse these two events—and it is easy to see why. In the Olivet discourse, Jesus goes back and forth between them, and if you do not read carefully, you might think He is describing one event. In one sense, He *is* describing one event: His *parousia*, His presence on earth. The *parousia* begins with His return to remove the church, and it climaxes with His glorious manifestation. So these two events are really different aspects of one *parousia*, one presence of the Lord Jesus Christ.

The first sentence of this section, however, makes it clear which aspect of His *parousia* presence the Lord is describing. At the beginning of the passage, He clearly states that His coming will be completely unpredictable: "No one knows about that day or hour, not even the angels in heaven, nor the Son, but only the Father." This description fits only one aspect of His *parousia*: The removal of the church, the Rapture. The unpredictable nature of this event is underscored by an additional warning Jesus makes later in the discourse.

> "Therefore keep watch, because you do not know on what day your Lord will come. But understand this: If the owner of the house had known at what time of night the thief was coming, he would have kept watch and would not have let his house be broken into. So you also must be ready, because the Son of Man will come at an hour when you do not expect him." (Matthew 24:42–44)

It would be impossible for Jesus to use these words in reference to His later coming in power and great glory at the end of the Great Tribulation. That event will not happen without warning. It will be preceded by numerous dramatic signs. As Jesus warned in Matthew 24:29, "the sun will be darkened, and the moon will not give its light; the stars will fall from the sky, and the heavenly bodies will be shaken." No person who understands the Scriptures could possibly miss those signs. Any believer who had seen those signs would expect the glorious appearance of Jesus at any moment. But here, in verse 44, Jesus tells His disciples, "the Son of Man will come at an hour when you do not expect him."

When Jesus comes to take His church out of the world His coming will be as a thief in the night. The church is the unsuspected treasure of earth, and He will come to take it to Himself. The world will have no inkling that it is about to occur. As Jesus has just said, we *can* know in a general and approximate sense that the time is drawing near because we can observe certain predicted patterns taking shape in human affairs. We can see ungodly attitudes emerging as the dominant philosophy of the day. We can see certain events taking place that suggest the end of the age is just over the horizon. But we cannot know the day or the hour. The angels do not know. Even the Son of Man, in the time of His earthly limitation, did not know. Only the Father knows.

The great Scottish minister, Horatio Bonar, once met with a number of fellow ministers. "Do you really expect Jesus Christ to come today?" he asked. One by one, he put that question to each minister around the circle. One by one, they shook their heads and said, "No, I don't expect Him to return today." Without comment, Bonar wrote some words on a piece of paper and passed it around the circle: "So you also must be ready, because the Son of Man will come at an hour when you do not expect him."

Jesus is coming suddenly, unexpectedly. In fact, Jesus compares His return to reclaim His church with a felonious act—a breaking and entering by a burglar. What a shocking comparison! Why does the Son of God compare Himself to a criminal? Because He is making a crucial point and He doesn't want the impact of that point to be lost.

Jesus is saying that if the homeowner had known when the thief was coming, he would have watched in readiness in order to prevent the robbery and catch the thief. If you know that on a given night, at a given hour, someone will enter your house to rob you, then you won't be caught napping—you'll be ready to nab a burglar! The problem with burglars is that they do not give advance notice. Burglars strike unexpectedly, without warning.

What is the only solution to the problem of burglars? Eternal vigilance. Constant readiness. Continual watchfulness. Never let your guard down. Never be caught napping. So, says Jesus, since you do not know when your Lord is coming, *be ready all the time.*

Does that mean we should stand on a rooftop, watching the skies for His return? Of course not. We have too much work to do, too many people to reach for Christ, too many wounded souls all around in need of His healing touch. Jesus told us, "Do you not say, 'Four months more and then the harvest'? I tell you, open your eyes and look at the fields! They are ripe for harvest." (John 4:35)

A white field of wheat is not merely ripe—it is overripe. Jesus is telling us that the work of the harvest is a crisis, it's an emergency. We don't have time to gaze foolishly into the skies when the work of the harvest is so urgent!

When Jesus tells us to be watchful and ready, He means that we should not be fooled by the deceitfulness of the age in which we live. We are surrounded by seductive lies. It is all part of the great satanic brainwashing campaign behind the philosophy of the world. If we fall for it, we will not be ready when He comes. The only defense against the satanic deception that surrounds us is a continuous, step-by-step reliance on the truth of God as illuminated for us by the indwelling Spirit of God.

Jesus said, "If you hold to my teaching, you are really my disciples. Then you will know the truth, and the truth will set you free" (John 8:31–32). The only defense against the world's deception is the Word of Truth. And the Word tells us that our duty is to serve God and others through an unceasing ministry of love and service in the name of Jesus Christ. Jesus said, "Occupy till I come" (Luke 19:13 KJV). In other words, "Remain at your post, do your duty, carry out your orders, and keep busy in the strength and the purpose of God."

Business as Usual

Even though Jesus has clearly said that He will return at a completely unexpected time, many Christians are obsessed with setting the date for His return. It doesn't seem to matter to them that their obsession is in direct violation of the Lord's own words. Again and again, down through history, we have seen religious leaders announce that the Lord's return would occur on such-and-such a date. Their followers sell their property, don white robes, and climb to some hilltop to await the Lord's appearance.

The result is that the entire subject of the return of Christ is made to look foolish! Though God's Word has a great deal to say about the Lord's return, God maintains an inscrutable silence about the exact timetable for that event. Jesus has told us that the day and the hour of His return are tucked away in a file marked TOP SECRET. As believers, we show disrespect for God by attempting to pry that file open, or by claiming to know its contents. As Jesus told His disciples after His resurrection, "It is not for you to know the times or dates the Father has set by his own authority" (Acts 1:7).

Jesus discourages date-setting. He encourages only one thing: *Continual readiness.* "So you also must be ready," He warns, "because the Son of Man will come at an hour when you do not expect him." We must be daily, hourly, momentarily prepared, because His return will be completely unexpected.

Jesus underscores the unexpected nature of His initial coming by comparing it to the days of Noah:

> "As it was in the days of Noah, so it will be at the coming of the Son of Man. For in the days before the flood, people were eating and drinking, marrying and giving in marriage, up to the day Noah entered the ark; and they knew nothing about what would happen until the flood came and took them all away. That is how it will be at the coming of the Son of Man." (Matthew 24:37–39)

Some Bible teachers have interpreted the Lord's reference to eating, drinking, and marriage as indicators of evil activity. Some have suggested that "eating" is a reference to increased gluttony throughout the earth, that "drinking" refers to rampant drunkenness and alcoholism, and "marrying and giving in marriage" refers to the climbing divorce rate. But there is not even the slightest hint of evidence that this is what Jesus is saying.

Elsewhere in the gospels, when Jesus wants to talk about gluttony, drunkenness, or divorce, He uses those precise terms. Here, He is not talking about moral vice or marital breakdown. He is talking about life as usual. He is saying that people will be going about their normal, everyday lives as they have always done—and in the blink of an eye, the whole world will change. Believers will be swept out of the world, and unbelievers will be left behind.

That is how it was in the days of Noah. Before the rain and the flood, life went on in an ordinary way. Yes, moral conditions were bad, and there was violence and corruption upon the earth. But those conditions had been going on for a long time—they didn't suddenly worsen just before the flood. Jesus is quite clear about this. He is saying simply that His coming will be sudden and unexpected, and the people of the world will be caught unsuspecting in the midst of their normal routines.

Of course, the people of Noah's day should have expected God's judgment. Noah was a tireless preacher, and he faithfully warned his generation that God would judge the world. He built his huge boat miles and miles from any ocean, and the people saw it and ridiculed him—then they went on about their normal lives. But when the rains came, Noah and his family were lifted safely above the floods while the rest of the world was left behind to drown in the waters of judgment.

The same is true today. The people of this world will have no excuse when Jesus comes for His church and they are left behind. Just as Noah preached to his generation, this generation has had many preachers. The gospel of Jesus Christ has gone out, the promise of His return has been broadcast far and wide. People hear it, they ridicule the message—then they go on about their normal lives. A day will come—and it will come unexpectedly—when Jesus will arrive to lift His church safely above the waters of God's judgment. In terms that are visual and unmistakable, Jesus describes what that moment will be like:

> "Two men will be in the field; one will be taken and the other left. Two women will be grinding with a hand mill; one will be taken and the other left." (Matthew 24:40–41)

Jesus Christ will come stealthily, without warning, like a thief in the night—and a select company will be removed from the earth. Those who are left behind will have no excuse. Like those who ridiculed Noah, they will have sealed their own judgment by their disobedience and unbelief.

Yearning For His Return

The event that Jesus describes will be highly selective, distinguishing even between two people who are working side by side. Further, it will be worldwide, for in the parallel passage in Luke 17:34, Jesus says, "I tell you, on that night two people will be in one bed; one will be taken and the other left." While men work in their fields on one side of the earth, others will be asleep in their beds on the other side. Simultaneously, across both the nightside and the dayside of the planet, a great removal will occur.

Most people believe that we enter life through the door marked BIRTH and we exit life through the door marked DEATH—that there is no other exit. But Jesus has shown us another door. On the

Mount of Transfiguration, the Lord showed Peter, James, and John that there is another way by which people can leave this life and enter glory. On that mountain, Jesus was suddenly transfigured before their astonished eyes. His clothing began to glow, and Jesus became a different person, though He was the same Jesus. The transfiguration of Jesus Christ was a foretaste of that great and wonderful mystery described by the apostle Paul:

> Listen, I tell you a mystery: We will not all sleep, but we will all be changed—in a flash, in the twinkling of an eye, at the last trumpet. For the trumpet will sound, the dead will be raised imperishable, and we will be changed. (1 Corinthians 15:51–52)

This event cannot be explained in natural terms. It is a miracle beyond human imagining. Some people might wish to "spiritualize" these words or treat them as a metaphor rather than a reality. But the Scriptures do not allow us to treat this event as anything other than a literal miracle that will envelop all believers, living and dead, at the moment of the Lord's return for His church. Again, Paul describes that event in clear, unambiguous language:

> For the Lord himself will come down from heaven, with a loud command, with the voice of the archangel and with the trumpet call of God, and the dead in Christ will rise first. After that, we who are still alive and are left will be caught up together with them in the clouds to meet the Lord in the air. And so we will be with the Lord forever. (1 Thessalonians 4:16–17)

There is a strange paradox in all of this: While we look for the Lord's return, He is already with us. While we await His *parousia*, He is already present. He is coming, yet He is with us now. There is great comfort in that truth.

Jesus never intended that we should live in fear of His return—yet many Christians do. I've known many believers who seem to think that awaiting the Lord's return means living in constant terror of making some brief slip, then having the Lord appear and say, "I caught you!" That is not the point of the Lord's warning. Jesus is not a motorcycle policeman, waiting behind a billboard, ready to surprise you in that unguarded moment when you drive three miles an hour over the speed limit. Jesus is our Lord, our Savior, our Redeemer, and our Friend.

Jesus wants us to know that there is a deep relationship between His presence with us now and His future coming. If we eagerly await His coming, if we look forward to His arrival with a sense of love and expectation, then we are experiencing His presence now. If we fear His coming, then we are not fully realizing and experiencing His presence in our lives. If the thought of His coming fills you with fear and apprehension, then you know little of His presence now. The heart that truly loves and serves Jesus is a heart that yearns for His return. ◇

10

Faithful and Unfaithful Servants

Matthew 24:45–51

An old woman walked into a little country store in the South. Several young men were loitering by the front counter, passing the time of day. Knowing that this woman was an outspoken Christian, they began to taunt her. "Hey, Mrs. Smith," they said, "we hear you're waiting for Jesus to come back."

"I sure am," the woman replied.

"When is He coming?" the young men asked.

"Could be today," she said. "Could be a hundred years from now."

"You really believe He's coming back after all these years?"

"As sure as you're born," she said.

"Well," the young men said, snickering, "you'd better hurry home and get ready. He might be on His way right now!"

The old woman turned a scolding look on the young men. "I don't have to get ready," she said, "I *keep* ready!"

That is the attitude Jesus wants us to have. In the next portion of the Olivet discourse, He presents three parables—three stories to illustrate what He means when He tells us to watch and wait for His return.

The first story He tells is the parable of the household, which teaches us that watching means a mutual concern and ministry of the Word to one another. The second is the parable of the ten virgins, which makes clear that watching means a dependence on deeper things than mere human resources. And the third is the parable of the talents, in which we learn that watching means a deliberate investment of ourselves.

In this chapter we will examine the first of these three parables from the prophecies of the Olivet discourse.

From Prediction to Parable

At this point the Lord has largely concluded the prophetic section of His discourse. Except for a few details concerning the final scene of the nations, there are no new events described in the rest of the message. But it is vital that we understand these three parables. These parables are the key to understanding our response to the Olivet prophecy. If we do not grasp their message, then we will not watch for Him in the way that He has called us to watch. And if we do not watch, we will be deceived. And if we are deceived, we will fail to lay hold of the exciting possibilities of the present and the wonders of the future.

He begins with the parable of the household:

> "Who then is the faithful and wise servant, whom the master has put in charge of the servants in his household to give them their food at the proper time? It will be good for that servant whose master finds him doing so when he returns. I tell you the truth, he will put him in charge of all his possessions." (Matthew 24:45–47)

This parable is intended for the instruction of those who await the Lord's return. The master of the household is gone, but he has entrusted certain work to his steward until he returns. That work is primarily a ministry to the rest of the household. Note that the master says the steward should "give them their food at the proper time."

Jesus clearly addresses this parable to His disciples and to all those who will follow in their footsteps—footsteps of ministry, of feeding and shepherding the church of Jesus Christ. It is addressed to everyone who has a ministry of teaching: pastors, evangelists, prophets, elders, Sunday school teachers, children's workers, and Bible class leaders. It includes all who have a spiritual gift of teaching, whether that gift is exercised in a church building, in a home, or on a street corner. It includes theological professors, editors of magazines, radio teachers, missionaries, youth workers, Christian authors, and many others.

Since this is the first parable in the series, it probably points up the most essential aspect of what it means to watch. The wise servant is given one primary responsibility: to feed the household at the proper time. If this duty is faithfully performed, the household will keep watching. If this duty is neglected, the household will languish and starve, and will not be ready when the Lord returns.

So the task of any Christian leader is to unfold the message of the Bible. Every pastor should set a table laden with spiritual nourishment before his congregation. His task is not merely to feed them but to show them how to feed themselves—that is, how to draw nourishment for themselves from the Scriptures. The Bible is wonderfully adapted to this purpose: There is milk for the beginner, bread for the more advanced, and strong meat to challenge and feed the mature. It is designed so that, when books of the Bible are taught in consecutive order, they cover a wide variety of subjects in a marvelous balance.

As the church awaits the return of the Lord, we need to feed ourselves and each other from the rich, nourishing food revealed to us in the Bible. From a deep knowledge of God's Word, all else will flow. The Bible is the revelation of things as they really are. It represents the only realistic look at life available to men and women today. It is the only instrument provided by God that is adequate for the task of producing mature, well-adjusted, whole persons. As Paul told his spiritual son Timothy:

> All Scripture is God-breathed and is useful for teaching, rebuking, correcting and training in righteousness, so that the man of God may be thoroughly equipped for every good work. (2 Timothy 3:16–17)

As we await the Lord's return, we must remain watchful, and we must remain in the Word of God. Above all, we must continually ask the Spirit of God to reveal the rich, living presence of Christ to us in its pages. That is how we feed on Him, and that is how we grow in Him.

The Incredible Reward

Imagine the joy of the faithful servant when his master returns and finds him conscientiously performing the task assigned to him. "It will be good for that servant," says Jesus, "whose master finds him doing so when he returns." What a joyful, satisfying feeling it will be to know that he did his work well in the eyes of the only one who counts. But that is not all that awaits the faithful servant. Jesus says there will also be an incredible reward for that servant.

"I tell you the truth," Jesus says, "he will put him in charge of all his possessions." In another place Jesus quotes the master as saying, "Well done, good and faithful servant! You have been faithful with a few things; I will put you in charge of many things. Come and share your master's happiness!" (Matthew 25:21). This is the invariable rule of the kingdom of God.

When you consider who this master really is, it is astounding to realize that Jesus intends to reward His faithful servants by setting them in authority over all of His possessions. Paul talks about that incredible reward in several places. To the Christians in Corinth, he wrote:

> All things are yours, whether Paul or Apollos or Cephas or the world or life or death or the present or the future—all are yours, and you are of Christ, and Christ is of God. (1 Corinthians 3:21–23)

In his letter to the Ephesians, Paul sums all of this up with the phrase, "the unsearchable riches of Christ" (Ephesians 3:8). Who can tell what wonders are embedded in those words? What boundless opportunities does God have planned for us? What indescribable adventures does He have in store? One thing is clear: For those who are faithful in the tasks He assigns in this life, amazing and unimaginable rewards are reserved in the life to come.

Best of all, the faithful servant of God will one day hear those thrilling words, "Well done, good and faithful servant! You have been faithful with a few things; I will put you in charge of many things. Come and share your master's happiness!"

The Unfaithful Servant

Unfortunately, not every servant of the Lord proves to be wise and faithful. With utter candor, Jesus also presents the negative side of the picture:

> "But suppose that servant is wicked and says to himself, 'My master is staying away a long time,' and he then begins to beat his fellow servants and to eat and drink with drunkards.

The master of that servant will come on a day when he does not expect him and at an hour he is not aware of. He will cut him to pieces and assign him a place with the hypocrites, where there will be weeping and gnashing of teeth." (Matthew 24:48–51)

The unfaithful servant has the same ministry as the faithful servant. He, too, was expected to care for the rest of the household and "give them their food at the proper time." The same storehouse of the Word is at his disposal. He has everything he needs to feed the household. The health and welfare of the household is his responsibility and depends on his faithful ministry.

But this servant has a different attitude toward his master and his own responsibility. When the master does not return as soon as he expects, this servant says to himself, "My master is staying away a long time." This is a key statement. It reflects a hint that the return of the Lord Jesus will be delayed far beyond people's expectations. The apostles expected Him in the first century, but He did not come. Centuries have elapsed. In each era, believers expected the Lord's imminent return—but He did not come back. After two thousand years, many have given up hope that He will ever return.

A bishop of a mainline Protestant church, who himself held no hope that Jesus would ever return, quoted a survey revealing that only 24 percent of his denomination believed in the literal return of Jesus Christ. Most members of that denomination had decided that the prophecy of Jesus was a failed prophecy, or that it had to be reinterpreted in some metaphoric sense. But, they concluded, Jesus would surely not return in any literal sense!

When people lose faith and hope in the reality of the Lord's return the effect is devastating. The servant, Jesus said, began to beat his fellow servants, mistreat them, neglect his ministry, and indulge his appetites to the full. It is a vivid picture of what happens, to one degree or another, when belief in the Lord's return is abandoned.

We can see a downward progression in the life of the unfaithful "Christian" who abandons belief in the Lord's return. The unfaithful "Christian" thinks, "My Master is gone, no one is watching, and it doesn't matter what I do—because who is going to stop me?" He neglects the ministry God has given him. He begins to mistreat others in the household of faith, the church. Instead of feeding the household, he feeds on worldly ideas and engages in worldly behavior with worldly people. Finally the Master returns— and the hypocritical, faithless, so-called "Christian" is assigned to the terrible fate he has earned: destruction.

Many people in this world call themselves "Christians," but the hope of the Christian, the hope of the Lord's return, does not live in them. The life of Christ does not exist in their lives. Outwardly they seem to be Christians, servants of the Lord. But inwardly they are unfaithful, and they will have much to be afraid of on the day their Master finally returns.

Clearly, the fact of Christ's return is a more important doctrine of the church than many people deem it to be. This doctrine is an indicator of the degree to which the Lord's indwelling presence is being experienced. The one with little desire for the Lord's return has little motivation to serve Him. When the inner hope of the Lord's return crumbles, all that remains is a hollow shell of pseudochristianity—a hypocritical pose that cannot withstand the pressures, trials, and temptations of life. That is why the Lord lays such stress upon His return. The loss of this hope is a primary cause of the neglect of Bible teaching in the church—and a church that neglects the Bible is a church that has become weakened to a fatal degree.

Though the servant has given up on the Lord's return, the Lord *will* return. He will appear on a day that the servant does not know, at an hour when the servant does not expect Him. Undoubtedly this will be one of those occasions when the servant will say, "Lord, Lord, have I not done mighty works in your name?" (see Matthew 7:22). He will try to impress the Lord with his accomplishments, but to no avail. He has not done what the Lord commanded him to do. He has not believed in the Lord's return, and he has not watched, waited, and served. He has been faithless to his commission. Therefore he shall be punished and put where he belongs—with the hypocrites! For that is what a hypocrite is—a person who plays the role of God's servant but who proves false to his trust.

It is clear from what our Lord says of this servant that he never was a true servant at all. Jesus is not saying that a genuine Christian can prove as false as this servant is. Yes, genuine Christians can stumble and fall—but they will not remain in a state of failure. Their hope in the Lord's return lifts them up and motivates them to return to the task that the Lord has given them. The one who abandons that hope and loses that motivation simply proves he never was a true Christian in the first place.

The Day Will Disclose It

The message of this parable is clear: It is a serious thing to neglect the feeding of the household of God. In many cases, the church today has lost its true identity, its sense of what God intended it to be. Instead of a body of believers who minister to one another in Christian love, the church has become an organization that merely operates programs.

Paul wrote to the Galatians, "Carry each other's burdens, and in this way you will fulfill the law of Christ" (Galatians 6:2). Tragically, Christians today often touch each other's lives in only the most superficial ways, and do not have the time or inclination to fulfill the law of Christ by bearing each other's burdens. "I don't need to get involved in my neighbor's needs, my neighbor's pain," we say. "Our church has programs for that."

The widespread ignorance of the church's true nature is directly traceable to a lack of systematic Bible teaching. The New Testament letters give us a detailed picture of what the life of the church should look like. The "body life" of the church is illustrated with actual events from first-century church history, and those events are as relevant today as they were two thousand years ago. The church's supernatural endowment with spiritual gifts for ministry is described in half a dozen places. The church's unique power, emanating from the presence of an indwelling and active Lord, is set before us throughout the New Testament. So, too, is the church's mission to make an impact on a decaying society.

But how much does the average Christian know of all of this? The blunt answer: Virtually nothing! The level of biblical illiteracy that prevails in many churches today is shocking and dismaying. The result is that we have a powerless, quarreling, materialistic church that is really little more than a worldly corporation. In such church organizations, the living presence of the Lord is practically unknown. And the hope of His return? Oh, that has long ago turned to dust and ashes.

What is the cause of all this sterile mediocrity in our churches? Jesus has given us the answer in this parable: It is faithless and wicked servants who have abandoned the hope of the Lord's return and have neglected the task of feeding the household. Jesus views this failure with the greatest solemnity. So we should not be surprised to hear Him say that when the master of the house returns, he will confront the faithless servant and will punish him and send him to his eternal fate among the hypocrites.

The day of the Lord's return reveals the true character of all His servants. The faithfulness of the good servant is revealed when the Master returns, and he receives an incredible reward. The hypocrisy of the faithless servant is also revealed when the Master returns, and he receives the eternal fate of all hypocrites. Every person's lifework, says the apostle Paul, "will be shown for what it is, because the Day will bring it to light" (1 Corinthians 3:13). For good or ill, what we are proved to be in that Day, we must continue to be forever! What we have been in the secret places of our lives must now be displayed as our true self throughout eternity.

So the Lord emphasizes that the present time is an exceedingly precious commodity. We must redeem these precious hours or lose them forever. The great missionary to Africa, C. T. Studd, summed up this truth in a profound couplet:

> Only one life, 'twill soon be past,
> Only what's done for Christ will last.

We easily lose sight of the irreplaceable nature of precious time. We tend to think that we have all the time in the world. One Bible scholar comments that we mistakenly see time as an endless, repetitive cycle. The reason we do not experience this more frequently is because our clocks are round. The hour hand starts at 12 and moves all the way around the dial, and starts over again at 12. So we think life is like that. We get up every morning, go to bed every night, and the next day it starts over again.

But on New Year's Eve, we discover otherwise. As the midnight hour approaches, we become quite aware that time is moving continually onward and we can never go back. Beginning with our birth, our lives move in a straight line until they end in death. Between those two points is a limited span of time. That is our allotment, no more, no less. When it is gone, our lives are done.

At certain points along that finite line of time, we experience milestones that remind us that life is not cyclical, it is linear. We experience birthdays, we watch the years accumulate, and we realize that life does not go on forever. Life is finite and brief. Each hour is precious and can never be repeated. The past is an unalterable fact. It can never be changed or repeated.

An hour approaches for us all when our one and only irreplaceable life has been lived. It will be impossible to go back and change it. For you, that moment will come either with your last heartbeat or with the return of the Master. Either way, you will have to account for the kind of servant you have been—faithful or faithless.

If you have been watching for your Lord's return, then the moment of final accounting holds no fear for you. In fact, you eagerly long for His return. That is the moment of supreme blessing for you, when you will be commended and rewarded, and you will see the face of the One you love.

But if you have not been waiting and watching, then that moment will be the most horrible experience imaginable.

What would you say if someone asked you, "How long have you lived?" You might say, "I'm _____ years old." But that would be the wrong answer. The question is not, "How old are you?" but "How long have you *lived*?" The only part of your existence that can truly be called *living* is the time you have spent watching and waiting for your Lord's return. That is the time you have truly served Him, truly gone about your tasks with a sense of love for Him and a desire to please Him. That is the only time you have truly been *alive*.

When are you going to start living? You only have today. ◇

11

The Wise and the Foolish

Matthew 25:1–13

Weddings never go out of style. They have been around since the beginning of the human race, and even after you have attended as many weddings as I have, there is still something fresh, beautiful, and moving about each one. We never seem to get over the excitement of watching two lives become one.

At every wedding, a lot of fuss is made over the bride and groom—and that's as it should be. This is their day! People rarely pay much attention to the attendants. But in His second parable in the Olivet discourse, Jesus chooses to focus on the attendants of a certain wedding. He chooses to use a wedding scene as the backdrop for a parable to illustrate what He means by the command, "Watch!" In this parable, Jesus doesn't even mention the bride, and the groom is referred to only incidentally. Here, Jesus directs our attention to ten attendants, ten young virgins who have been invited to the wedding.

Although we have come to a chapter division at this point, there is no break in the flow of the Lord's Olivet discourse. This point in the text should be viewed as a seamless transition from the first to the second of three parables, all of which arise from the prophetic message He has just unveiled for us in Matthew 24. The theme of this second parable is twofold: (1) the unexpectedness of the Lord's return for His church, and (2) the need to continue watching and waiting for His return.

The phrase that links this parable to the prophetic one before it is "At that time." Jesus introduces the parable of the ten virgins: "At that time the kingdom of heaven will be like ten virgins. . . ." At what time? At the time of Jesus Christ's return as a thief in the night before the Great Tribulation. At that time, He will appear on an unexpected day, at an unknown hour.

The linkage of this parable in Matthew 25 to the preceding discussion in Matthew 24 is made still more clear when the Lord adds (as He also said in the previous chapter), "Therefore keep watch, because you do not know the day or the hour" (Matthew 25:13).

The Expected Bridegroom

Let's now join Jesus as He relates the second parable to His disciples on the Mount of Olives:

> "At that time the kingdom of heaven will be like ten virgins who took their lamps and went out to meet the bridegroom. Five of them were foolish and five were wise. The foolish ones took their lamps but did not take any oil with them. The wise, however, took oil in jars along with their lamps. The bridegroom was a long time in coming, and they all became drowsy and fell asleep.
>
> "At midnight the cry rang out: 'Here's the bridegroom! Come out to meet him!'

"Then all the virgins woke up and trimmed their lamps. The foolish ones said to the wise, 'Give us some of your oil; our lamps are going out.'" (Matthew 25:1–7)

There is more to the story, of course, but those seven verses serve as an introduction. The setting is a wedding in the ancient Middle East. In that culture, the bridegroom, not the bride, was the focus of the attention. In that culture, the bridegroom bore all the expense of the wedding, and he was the most visible part of the wedding celebration. Weddings were always held at night. It was customary for the bridegroom to go to the house of the bride and take her to the wedding. As they walked through the streets they would be joined by guests along the route. Our Lord's story of the ten virgins is the account of one such group.

The story is intended for those who live in that period of time before the Lord's first coming and His second. The parable makes sense only if we are able to recognize ourselves in its cast of characters. Jesus is telling us how we are to watch and wait for His return.

The First Movement: A Common Expectation

There are five movements in this story. The first movement is one of a *common expectation*. Here is a group of people at a wedding, waiting for the bridegroom's arrival. Life consists of a great deal of waiting. As children, we can't wait to grow up and be on our own. As young adults, we can't wait to find that special someone so that we can get married. When we get married, we can hardly wait to have children. And those children? They can't wait to grow up and be on their own! And so it goes.

We tend to think of waiting as a dreary and unpleasant experience—for example, waiting in the dentist's office until it's our turn to go under the drill. But the kind of waiting that this story describes is a happy, excited, expectant waiting—like waiting for the birth of a child or waiting for Christmas. Some things in life are worth waiting for. The joy that lies at the end of a period of anticipation can transform waiting into a sweet and wonderful experience. If nothing is worth waiting for, life becomes a colorless existence.

These ten virgins were waiting for the coming of the bridegroom. They symbolize believers who wait for the coming of Jesus Christ. Throughout this discourse, we have listened to the words of the greatest Prophet who ever lived. We have heard His astounding prophecy. We are convinced that history will culminate in the appearance of the One who has spoken these words. We share, along with these ten virgins, a common expectation of the coming of the Bridegroom.

The Second Movement: Wise and Foolish

But there is a line of division that runs down the middle of this group of young women. Five are on one side of this line, five are on the other. And therein lies the second movement of this parable. Here is what Jesus says about these virgins:

> "Five of them were foolish and five were wise. The fool-
> ish ones took their lamps but did not take any oil with them.
> The wise, however, took oil in jars along with their lamps."
> (Matthew 25:2–4)

These ten young women are united in their expectation of the bridegroom. They are quite divided, however, in the way that each group of five chooses to wait for him. Five virgins have brought along extra oil; five have not. It is important to understand that Jesus is not making a distinction between people who are good and bad, but between the wise and the foolish. There is no moral distinction intended here. In their anticipation of the coming bridegroom, all of these ten virgins are equally sincere and devoted. The only difference is that five of them knew that it would be wise to bring along extra oil for their lamps.

This proves to be the most significant part of the story. To the five foolish virgins, this was a trivial matter. The important thing was that the bridegroom was coming. It didn't occur to them that they might run out of oil for their lamps, and they made no preparation. They all agreed that oil was important, and they agreed that the purpose for having lamps filled with oil was to provide light. But the five wise virgins had the foresight to realize that the bridegroom might come late, so extra lamp oil might be needed in order to provide light for a greater length of time.

What does the oil represent? We shall examine that aspect of the story in a moment. What is evident at this point is that this story is highly relevant to our own time. There are wise and foolish people in the church today. We agree that we expect the bridegroom to come. But some of us who have that expectation are wise, while others are foolish. To be foolish, as we shall see, means to lack that which is essential for waiting until the Lord returns. To be wise is to have something that is symbolized for us by the extra lamp oil.

Seemingly, everything would have gone well for all ten virgins if the bridegroom had come when he was expected. The problem arose because there was a delay. This delay underscored the difference between the wise and foolish virgins. The wise had something the foolish did not. What is that essential thing that separates the wise from the foolish? Jesus gives us some important clues in the parable.

The Third Movement: The Delay

The third movement of the story introduces the element of delay: The bridegroom does not arrive when he is expected. Jesus says:

> "The bridegroom was a long time in coming, and they all became drowsy and fell asleep.
>
> "At midnight the cry rang out: 'Here's the bridegroom! Come out to meet him!'" (Matthew 25:5–6)

Jesus does not explain why the bridegroom was delayed. This element of the story seems to be another hint from the Lord that His absence would be long extended, as has certainly proved to be the case. It was the delay of the bridegroom that created an unexpected demand on the part of the ten virgins for more oil. By the time the bridegroom arrived, the oil in the lamps had been used up, and the lamps were running dry. More oil was needed. During the long wait, all ten virgins had grown tired and had fallen asleep.

Some Bible teachers have suggested that this meant that the virgins were negligent. However, I cannot find even a hint of rebuke or disapproval as Jesus relates this story. He does not seem to think the virgins were negligent for sleeping. Note that the wise fell asleep along with the foolish. Sleep is a perfectly natural and right thing to do, under the circumstances. People need rest. It was night and there was no work to be done, so why shouldn't they sleep?

I believe Jesus wants us to understand that watching and waiting doesn't mean that we are to be in a constant state of high-strung tension and anxiety. He does not want us to scan the skies continuously as if we were air-raid wardens awaiting an attack by enemy bombers! We are to go about our normal lives—earning a living, raising our families, enjoying our lives and our leisure time, and yes, resting when we are tired.

While these wise and foolish virgins were sleeping, they were engaged in one of the normal, necessary activities of life. Even as they slept, these virgins were waiting for the bridegroom's coming. Their activity (or rather, their inactivity) was a perfectly proper use of their time.

Here Comes the Bridegroom

But suddenly there came a cry of warning: "Here's the bridegroom! Come out to meet him!" At the sound of that cry, all ten of the young women awoke. Clearly, the problem that the foolish virgins faced had nothing to do with the fact that they had fallen asleep. They awoke in plenty of time to meet the bridegroom.

This symbolizes the way life will be for those believers who are alive when the Lord returns for His church. The cry that these young virgins hear may be a symbol of the shout of the returning Lord when He comes for us. The apostle Paul tells us that when He comes, He will come with a shout (see 1 Thessalonians 4:16). The words of that shout may indeed be, "The Bridegroom is here! Come out to meet Him!"

The Fourth Movement: Inadequate Resources

The fourth movement of the story brings a crisis. This crisis reveals the wisdom of the wise—and the foolishness of the foolish:

"Then all the virgins woke up and trimmed their lamps. The foolish ones said to the wise, 'Give us some of your oil; our lamps are going out.'

"'No,' they replied, 'there may not be enough for both us
and you. Instead, go to those who sell oil and buy some for
yourselves.'" (Matthew 25:7–9)

The bridegroom has arrived, and the foolish maidens are dis-
mayed to discover that their lamps are flickering and about to go
out! The lamps have been burning while they slept, and the long
delay has used up the oil in the lamps. So they make an appeal to
the wise virgins. "Give us some of your oil," they plead. "Our
lamps are going out." The wise virgins reply that oil is not something that can be borrowed or lent, which suggests that whatever
the oil symbolizes, it is an individual matter.

I have experienced times of crisis when I found that my inner
resources were simply not equal to the demand. I'm sure you have
known times like that as well. Sometimes we see people undergoing terrible crises, and we think, *That situation would destroy me—
but they are going through it with such peace and strength! How do they
do it?* We wish we could borrow some of that person's strength, but
we can't. In the hour of trial, we each have only what we have and
nothing more.

So it is with these five foolish virgins. Their oil is gone and they
are in a panicky rush to get more. But they can't borrow more oil.
They have what they have and nothing more. They were not prepared for the time of trial.

The Fifth Movement: The Bridegroom's Denial

Jesus continues the story, bringing us to the fifth and final movement. This movement deals with the bridegroom's denial of the
foolish virgins:

"But while they were on their way to buy the oil, the bridegroom arrived. The virgins who were ready went in with him to the wedding banquet. And the door was shut.

"Later the others also came. 'Sir! Sir!' they said. 'Open the door for us!'

"But he replied, 'I tell you the truth, I don't know you.'

"Therefore keep watch, because you do not know the day or the hour." (Matthew 25:10–13)

Unable to borrow oil, the foolish virgins go out to buy some. While they are gone, the bridegroom arrives. All that waiting—and they miss the arrival of the very one they were waiting for! When they finally get back, they find the door shut. Do you find that surprising, even disturbing? Do you feel that the five foolish young women were unjustly treated? Why shouldn't they be allowed into the wedding? They were just a few minutes late. That seems so unfair—but is it?

Look closely at the Lord's words. There is not trace of vindictiveness in the shut door. The bridegroom doesn't say, "Let that be a lesson to you! That's what you get for being late!" No, he says, "I tell you the truth, I don't know you." The bridegroom sincerely and truthfully does not know these young women.

We must be careful that we do not impose our fallible judgment on the righteous and wise teaching of our Lord. What the Lord does and says is always right, so when He says something that is difficult for us to accept, we must look closer and study the clues so that we can understand His actions.

Notice, first, that there is a note of sorrow in the bridegroom's words: "I tell you the truth, I don't know you." Our Lord's words are a faithful, honest revelation of something that has been true all along. A wedding is no place for strangers. Only the friends of the two families are permitted to come. The door is shut and these five foolish virgins can't enter—and with good reason. They are strangers. The bridegroom doesn't know them.

The Meaning of Oil

Now we come to a question that has likely been bothering you for a while: What does the oil represent? Clearly, it signifies something of crucial importance for our lives—but what? Let's take a closer look at the words of the Lord. As we follow the clues, the mystery will soon become clear.

We know that there must be a connection between the foolish virgins' lack of oil and the fact that the bridegroom told them, "I don't know you." It is the lack of oil that causes them to be shut out of the wedding, so there must be some sense in which the lack of oil reveals them as strangers to the wedding celebration.

Oil, in the Old Testament, is frequently used as a symbol of the Holy Spirit. Kings and priests were anointed with oil to signify that they were to live consecrated and Spirit-filled lives (though many of those kings grievously violated that symbol!). The prophet Zechariah was shown a vision of a great golden lampstand with two olive trees standing beside it. The trees dripped oil into the bowls of the lampstand, and Zechariah was told: "'Not by might nor by power, but by my Spirit,' says the LORD Almighty" (Zechariah 4:6). The oil symbolized the Spirit of God by which the light of testimony could be maintained in the hour of darkness.

So in the symbol of the oil, we catch a glimpse of the ministry of the Holy Spirit. The central ministry of the Spirit is to impart the knowledge of Jesus Christ to men and women. Jesus Himself explained the ministry of the Spirit in these words:

"But when he, the Spirit of truth, comes, he will guide you into all truth. He will not speak on his own; he will speak only what he hears, and he will tell you what is yet to come. He will bring glory to me by taking from what is mine and making it known to you." (John 16:13–14)

The Spirit's task is to reveal Jesus Christ to us through the Word of God. There are various levels of revelation. There is even a Spirit-born ministry of the Word to those who are not true Christians. Jesus said that when the Holy Spirit comes, "he will convict the world of guilt in regard to sin and righteousness and judgment" (John 16:8). The Spirit will perform this ministry in the life of any person who will honestly seek the truth in the Scriptures. Those who respond to the convicting ministry of the Spirit, those who open their hearts and receive Jesus as Lord and Savior, will then be indwelt by the Spirit. The Spirit who first brought conviction of sin will then bring the light of wisdom, knowledge, and insight that comes as the Spirit takes the believer deeper and deeper into an experience with the living Christ.

We should never be satisfied with a merely intellectual portrait of Christ. The goal of our study of God's Word should always be a deeper level of relationship to the living Lord. It is possible to know a great deal of doctrine and not know the Lord. It is possible to commit long passages of Scripture to memory and not know the Lord. It is possible to become immersed in religious service and religious activity and not know the Lord.

That is the problem with the foolish virgins. They gladly took enough oil of the Spirit to give them a temporary "religious experience," or help with a difficulty, or temporary relief from guilt. But they didn't take sufficient oil to maintain their light until the bridegroom's arrival.

Let's unveil the symbols and speak plainly: These foolish virgins represent people who have received just enough of the Christian "religion" to have a little temporary light. Outwardly they may be indistinguishable from authentic Christians who are indwelt by the Spirit and whose light will never go out. But inwardly they are not authentic. They may seem "religious." They may know a lot of "religious" talk. They may do a lot of "religious" works. When Jesus returns, He will look upon them with genuine sorrow and sadness, and He will say to them, "I tell you the truth, I don't know you."

The foolish virgins represent those who have nothing more than a superficial or intellectual knowledge of God, of Jesus, of the truth. They may have all the right doctrines, but they do not have Jesus. They may have read the Word of God, but they do not have the Spirit of God living in them, giving them the light of understanding. They may have orthodox knowledge, but they have never experienced a genuine relationship with Jesus of Nazareth, Jesus the Christ, Jesus the Lord. Knowledge is worthless unless it leads to the surrender of self.

God freely lights a lamp of knowledge for all who want to know His truth. But Jesus indicates that something deeper than knowledge is needed—a deeper level of commitment to the Spirit of God, a sense of moment-by-moment reliance upon the Spirit for the power to meet the demands that life unexpectedly thrusts upon us.

Those who are wise have found a deeper level of reliance upon the Spirit of God. They have found a deeper experience with Jesus Christ. They do not just have a religion. They have a reservoir of oil that continually feeds the flame of life, even in the hour of darkness and trial. They have a supply of supernatural oil that lights the flame of life despite the most trying circumstances. The greater the pressures and stresses of life, the brighter the light shines.

I once called on a man in the hospital. He had been a Christian for many years. He sat up in bed, his body wasted away to a skeleton. He was unable to move a muscle, even to lift his arms or turn his head. He could no longer speak. I asked him if he would like me to read the Scriptures to him and he nodded his head yes. As I read, I watched his eyes. As the marvelous words from Isaiah melted into his soul, I saw a flame come alight in his eyes. Before our time was over, I saw in that emaciated body the glory of a burning flame—unquenchable, inexhaustible, fed by the oil of the Spirit.

There was no doubt in my mind—he was one of the wise. He had a rich supply of the oil of the Spirit. When he arrived at the wedding celebration, he would find the door open, the bridegroom greeting him with a smile of recognition.

That is the meaning of the symbol of the oil.

Renounce—or Risk Everything!

When life is easy and problems are few, people often tell themselves, "I don't have any need of extra reserves. A little religion is all I need. I don't need to surrender to God's Spirit. I don't need a deep relationship with Jesus Christ. I'm doing okay."

But what if trials come? What if the pressures and stresses of this life become too much for you to bear? Or what if that little bit of religion that is "enough" right now turns out to be of no real value in your life, and you find yourself drifting into darkness and coldness and worldliness? What will you do then?

In every life, a time comes when you realize it is late. The bridegroom has come. Either you are prepared and ready, with reserves of oil to light your way—or you find your lamp is empty and your light is flickering. When that moment comes, it is no good to turn to the person next to you and beg for "oil." It can't be done. The "oil" of God's Spirit cannot be transferred from one person to another. It cannot be begged or borrowed. When the time comes, you either have that "oil" or you don't. You have either taken God seriously during the time of waiting or you haven't. You have either been wise, or you've been foolish.

Have you taken God seriously? Have you taken Jesus Christ seriously when He said that He is the way, the truth, and the life, and that no one comes to the Father but through the Son? It has been said that there are only two ways to take something seriously: (1) you can renounce it in all seriousness, or (2) you can risk everything on it. This is what Jesus meant when He said, "For whoever wants to save his life will lose it, but whoever loses his life for me will find it" (Matthew 16:25). He is saying, "When you come to Me, you must risk everything on Me. If you want eternal life, you must cast everything you are and everything you have on Me."

Some want a third choice. They want to make a partial commitment, a compromise arrangement with God. They want to subscribe to the truth of Scripture but they don't want it to interfere with the way they live their lives. They want God to be an add-on to the plans they have already made.

But God will not be an add-on; you must either take Him as your absolute sovereign Lord or you must reject Him. He accepts no compromises. A third alternative simply does not exist. That is what Jesus is telling us in the parable of the wise and foolish virgins. That is why He says plainly to the foolish virgins, "I tell you the truth, I don't know you."

The end of the parable reveals the foolish virgins for what they are: They are strangers and outcasts. The door is shut to them, just as it is shut to the unbeliever. The unbeliever has rejected Jesus outright. But the foolish person tries to have it both ways. He tries to get into the wedding without the oil of God's Spirit. He tries to compromise.

The foolish person has no place at the wedding because that person never took God seriously. May God save you and me from this folly. ◇

12

Living Dangerously

Matthew 25:14–30

The Adventure of the Engineer's Thumb is a detective mystery by Sir Arthur Conan Doyle, one of the many stories showcasing the brilliant investigative skills of Sherlock Holmes. In that story, Holmes' friend, Dr. Watson, describes the process by which the great detective achieves his amazing results: "The facts slowly evolve before your own eyes," said Watson, "and the mystery clears gradually away as each new discovery furnishes a step which leads on to the complete truth."

I think it is fascinating that the very same statement could be made about the parables of Jesus.

Parables can be as exciting and challenging as detective stories. In fact, the parables of our Lord are even *more* exciting and challenging than mere fiction, because they deal with the most important issues of real life, while crime thrillers and mysteries can sometimes be rather far-fetched. Like detective stories, parables are filled with half-hidden truths and secret meanings, yet the clues to unraveling these real-life mysteries are always there to be found if you look carefully. Parables are God's exciting way of challenging us to hunt for His clues. The treasure we seek is a new insight into the nature of life—an insight that will enrich us in a thousand ways if we build its hidden truths into our lives.

Now we come to the third and final parable of the Olivet discourse, the parable of the talents. Again, the point of this story is
to illustrate what Jesus means when He commands us to watch and
wait for His return. The opening words of this parable link it to the
previous two parables and to the rest of the Olivet prophecy. This
parable is structured on the same basic pattern as the previous two:
The master goes away and leaves a group of people to fulfill a certain task until he returns. Here is the introduction to the parable:

> "Again, it will be like a man going on a journey, who
> called his servants and entrusted his property to them. To one
> he gave five talents of money, to another two talents, and to
> another one talent, each according to his ability. Then he
> went on his journey. The man who had received the five tal-
> ents went at once and put his money to work and gained five
> more. So also, the one with the two talents gained two more.
> But the man who had received the one talent went off, dug a
> hole in the ground and hid his master's money." (Matthew
> 25:14–18)

In some ways, this is a deeply puzzling parable. The central
question, of course, is: What do the talents represent?

Pitfalls of the Parable

A common but superficial understanding of this parable interprets
it as meaning that we need to put our natural gifts and abilities to
work for God. Someone says, "I play the piano, so I would like to
devote my talent to the Lord." Another says, "I have a gift for
teaching, so I would like to develop that talent and devote it to
Christ." These interpretations miss the real point of the parable.

The pitfall of this parable is that word *talent*. We are easily misled by the modern definition of that word, because the ancient meaning was quite different. To us, a talent is a natural ability, an aptitude, a capacity for performance, even a kind of genius. But in biblical times, a talent (from the Greek word *talanton*) was a unit of weight used as a medium of exchange throughout ancient Greece, Rome, and the Middle East. When Jesus used the word *talent* in the Olivet discourse, His disciples thought of it as a definite amount of money, a specific weight of silver, valued at around one thousand dollars. The idea that a talent was an ability, such as a musical talent, never entered their thoughts.

It is true that the Lord uses the image of a talent of silver—a specific amount of money—to represent something non-material in our lives. But He did not have natural abilities in mind when He told the parable of the talents. In fact, we shall see in a moment why the talents in this story could not possibly represent the kinds of talents we normally associate with that word.

The question before us is this: What has the Lord given to us to invest? What are our God-given "talents" that correspond to the talents of silver given to the servants in the parable?

What Do the Talents Represent?

Another pitfall of this parable is the risk of interpreting it as though it deals merely in ultimate rewards for service. This mistaken interpretation often accompanies the idea that the talents represent natural gifts. Here is how this view mistakenly interprets the parable: "We must use our natural gifts to the full for Christ, because if we do not, we may lose our reward—though of course, we will not lose our salvation."

This is a complete misunderstanding of the crucial message Jesus wants us to understand. In fact, our salvation is the very thing that is at stake in this parable! Jesus is warning us that our ultimate destiny as professed servants of Christ is very much at issue. The last line of the story makes this fact abundantly clear. Of the man with one talent, the returned master says, "And throw that worthless servant outside, into the darkness, where there will be weeping and gnashing of teeth." The final scene reveals that the worthless servant was not really a Christian at all.

Clearly, "talents" (that is, what these talents of silver symbolize in our lives) are distributed not only to true believers but are also given to false believers as well. "Talents" are given to all who *claim* to be servants of the Lord. What people do with these "talents" is an exceedingly vital issue. A person's eternal destiny depends on the matter. It is a question of eternal life or eternal death.

We must look for ourselves in this parable if we are to see what Jesus intends for our lives. In Mark's account of this same parable (see Mark 13:32–37), the Lord says, "What I say to you [the disciples], I say to everyone: 'Watch!'" (Mark 13:37). This parable is addressed to any who have any interest in the ultimate outcome of history as Jesus describes it. The Lord has distributed one or more "talents" to everyone who has investigated the issue of His return. We are either trading with it and investing it, or we are burying it in the ground. That is the central issue.

What, then, do "talents" represent in our own lives? Jesus gives us several clues.

The first hint is found in the opening verse, Matthew 25:14: "Again, it will be like a man going on a journey, who called his servants and entrusted his property to them." Note these two crucial words: "his property." That is another term for the talents which are distributed. They represent God's property, something that belongs entirely to the Lord. Whatever the talents signify, we know it is *not* something that we possess or control. It is not something that is ours to give. It is something that comes from God and only He can control. Whatever these talents are, they are not freely distributed, like natural gifts, to all people. They are given only to people who, in some way, have a relationship to God—the relationship of a servant. God distributes His property to those who claim to be His servants.

The second clue is found in the next verse: "To one he gave five talents of money, to another two talents, and to another one talent, each according to his ability." Note that last phrase: "each according to his ability." Here we learn that the "talents" Jesus speaks of are *not* natural abilities, for they are actually distributed on the *basis* of natural ability. To one man, the Lord gave five talents because he was a man of great natural ability. He had many natural gifts. To another he gave two talents because he was not as gifted as the first. To the third man he only gave one talent because he had few natural abilities.

The third clue is not stated in the text but is clearly implied. It is the unspoken implication that the Lord expected these servants to invest the talents given them to produce a gain, a return on investment. The talent, then, is something that can be invested and risked, with the possibility of producing gain or loss. The decision to risk is wholly the servant's. He can choose to take this risk, as the first two servants did, or he can utterly refuse to do so, as the third one did.

The fourth clue is the fact that the investment must be made wholly for the benefit of the absent Lord. The talent is not given to the servant for his own use. It remains the property of his absent Lord. If it is risked, it must be on the Lord's behalf. There is no promise made to the servants that they will share in any way in the profits. They have no right to deduct a broker's percentage. As far as the servant could see, all the loss would be his, all the profit would be the master's.

The Riddle Solved

Now, let's sum up these four clues and ask ourselves: What do we, as professed Christians, have that is God's own property? What is it that we receive on the basis of natural ability, which requires a risk on our part, and the investment of which benefits only the Lord and not ourselves? Can you answer that?

Look at it this way: When you know you have certain natural abilities, what do you do? You look for *opportunities* to use those gifts. The more talents we feel we have, the more we look for occasions to express them.

So the talents of this parable represent *golden moments of opportunity*. Just as money and property belong to human masters and is theirs to distribute as they see fit, so time and opportunities belong to God and are His to bestow or withhold according to His sovereign will.

Don't you find this very principle at work in your life? I certainly do in mine. As we look back over our lives, we find that there are times when we have struggled to express some natural ability, only to be frustrated again and again. We think we have something to offer, but we meet only brick walls and slammed doors. When the opportunity to express that gift finally comes our way, it comes in a manner that is completely beyond our control—what some would call a "lucky break." But the Christian knows there is no such thing as "luck." It is God who dispenses these opportunities according to His own sovereign will.

And what about the "bad breaks" in life? What about those times when our best efforts to use our gifts end in defeat and discouragement? What about those times when the opportunity we seek is withdrawn from us? Who governs these opportunities? Do you not agree that these opportunities are something that God alone withholds? We may think we have something to offer, but God sees the future and knows all circumstances. When He withholds an opportunity it is because He has something better planned for us. Opportunities are His property to distribute as He pleases, according to His sovereign will.

It is clear from this story that such opportunities come on the basis of how many natural gifts we possess. Every day we see examples of extremely gifted people who abound in opportunities to demonstrate what they can do. For those less gifted, opportunities come less often. And for some people, there is that once-in-a-lifetime Cinderella opportunity to step into the limelight and display that hidden ability.

Jesus is telling us that opportunities are given on the basis of natural gifts. Our response is to invest those chances in order to bring the greatest possible reward and return to our Master when He arrives.

Opportunities to display abilities and gifts come to all kinds of people, Christian or not. But opportunities that bring gain to Christ come only to professed Christians. These situations present us with moments of decision: We can play it safe and get what we can for ourselves—or we can risk reputation, possessions, and life itself so that God may have what He wants. These opportunities are the times when we cast the die of our lives for an ultimate good or an ultimate evil.

Such moments can occur when we are confronted with moral choices. "Should I yield to my passions and do what is wrong? Or should I be true to God? If I do what is wrong, I may gain pleasure, possessions, a promotion, or other advantages. If I do what God wants me to do, I take a risk—I may lose everything so that God can gain more glory. Which shall I choose?"

At other times, those moments of opportunity may not involve a moral choice but simply the question of where our gifts will be exercised. For example: "Should I respond to this opportunity to invest my life as a social worker in a slum area for Christ's sake—or should I play it safe and continue my plans to be a rich lawyer?" There is nothing morally wrong with a career in law—but if God presents us with an opportunity for service and we *bury* that opportunity, what kind of servants are we?

Or: "Should I take the time to teach this home Bible class with its life-changing possibilities—or should I go on reserving each Tuesday night for an evening out with friends?" There is nothing morally wrong with spending time with friends; in fact, our friendships often provide important opportunities for ministry and witness—but if God presents us with an opportunity for service and we *bury* that opportunity, what kind of servants are we?

Or: "Should I get involved with my neighbor's seemingly endless problems and help her find her hope in God—or should I play it safe, not get involved, and simply use that time in a way that gratifies and enriches my own life?" There is nothing morally wrong with reserving time for ourselves and our own enrichment—but if God brings us an opportunity to serve others and we turn our backs on it, what kind of servants are we?

These God-given opportunities are part of the life of everyone who professes to be a Christian. They are distributed to each of us according to our ability. There will inevitably be an accounting before God, when He will ask us how we invested these opportunities He has given us.

The Accounting

The master distributes the talents, then he leaves. While he is gone, the servants invest those talents as they see fit. Finally, the master returns and each servant is called to give an accounting. Here Jesus describes that day of reckoning:

> "After a long time the master of those servants returned and settled accounts with them. The man who had received the five talents brought the other five. 'Master,' he said, 'you entrusted me with five talents. See, I have gained five more.'
>
> "His master replied, 'Well done, good and faithful servant! You have been faithful with a few things; I will put you in charge of many things. Come and share your master's happiness!'" (Matthew 25:19–21)

This first servant has gained a 100 percent return. He has made *full use of his opportunities*, not for his own advancement but for his master's. Translating this parable into its meaning for our lives, he made each decision about the investment of his opportunities in light of what would advance the work of Christ. He risked great loss to himself in order that Jesus the Lord might gain. He took a chance that he might never have a place of prominence, influence, or power, but deliberately invested his opportunity along a line that would give God what He wanted. He ministered to the brokenhearted, provided comfort for the fatherless and afflicted, brought liberty to the captives, and proclaimed the gospel to the poor.

In effect, this servant placed *all* of his God-given opportunities at Christ's service. In response, Jesus said, "Well done, good and faithful servant!" Jesus Christ would never say "well done" unless it had truly been well done. This is not empty praise, rendered meaningless by being spoken to everyone alike regardless of performance.

This was authentic affirmation, and the Lord follows these words by granting the servant increased authority over many things. He adds these words: "Come and share your master's happiness."

What is that happiness? The book of Hebrews tells us to set our eyes upon Jesus, "who for the joy set before him endured the cross, scorning its shame, and sat down at the right hand of the throne of God" (Hebrews 12:2). Our master's happiness is nothing less than the joy of achieving the task that God has set before us, the joy of having satisfied the heart of God. It is an eternal joy that never fades, as earthly pleasures do, but which remains fresh and thrilling throughout eternity.

Jesus continues the story of the final accounting, as the master moves on to the second servant in line:

> "The man with the two talents also came. 'Master,' he said, 'you entrusted me with two talents; see, I have gained two more.'
>
> "His master replied, 'Well done, good and faithful servant! You have been faithful with a few things; I will put you in charge of many things. Come and share your master's happiness!'" (Matthew 25:22–23)

The servant with two talents had gained two talents more. Had he accomplished less than the first servant? Well, yes and no. The first servant had gained five talents, and the second had gained only two—but *both* servants had made a 100 percent return on their master's investment! What is Jesus telling us by this fact? Something quite significant: Both servants performed to the very limit of their ability. Both produced a 100 percent return on investment. The second man started with less, and produced a smaller return, but both had put out the maximum effort and both received the maximum return. Both risked loss to themselves so that their master might prosper.

The second servant received a commendation just as the first servant did. The master's message to the second servant was identical to his commendation of the first, word for word: "Well done, good and faithful servant! You have been faithful with a few things; I will put you in charge of many things. Come and share your master's happiness!"

You might ask what the additional talents—the return on the servants' investments—represents. Put another way, what does the profit symbolize? If the original talents represent opportunities for expressing our abilities in the cause of Christ, then the added talents, the increase from the investments, must represent more opportunities on a different level, in a higher realm. I think it very likely that the talents gained represent opportunities to invest spiritual gifts—those gifts of the Spirit listed in 1 Corinthians 12 and Romans 12, gifts that are given to every true Christian without exception.

If this is so, then the reward that the Master gives His servants would consist of new opportunities earned—the right to exercise spiritual power and make a spiritual impact on lives. Again and again, I've heard of Christians who have discovered a spiritual gift only when they have seized an occasion to be used by the Master, Jesus Christ. They have to decided to risk, to venture forth, for His sake. They may feel ill-equipped and clumsy at first, and they may have a complete lack of confidence. But they seize the God-given opportunity and do what needs to be done. As God works through them, they find a gift for ministry that they never knew they had—a newly discovered gift of the Spirit.

When we risk, when we courageously seize the opportunities God gives us, our investment is returned to Him and we discover a sense of the Spirit's empowerment that we never suspected was there before. When that happens, we enter into the joy and happiness of Jesus.

No Risk, No Gain—Only Loss

Inexorably, Jesus moves toward the tragic climax of His story. One servant remains to give his accounting:

> "Then the man who had received the one talent came. 'Master,' he said, 'I knew that you are a hard man, harvesting where you have not sown and gathering where you have not scattered seed. So I was afraid and went out and hid your talent in the ground. See, here is what belongs to you.'
>
> "His master replied, 'You wicked, lazy servant! So you knew that I harvest where I have not sown and gather where I have not scattered seed? Well then, you should have put my money on deposit with the bankers, so that when I returned I would have received it back with interest.
>
> "Take the talent from him and give it to the one who has the ten talents. For everyone who has will be given more, and he will have an abundance. Whoever does not have, even what he has will be taken from him. And throw that worthless servant outside, into the darkness, where there will be weeping and gnashing of teeth.'" (Matthew 25:24–30)

This may seem to be unduly strict treatment for the servant with one talent. He at least had the sense to bury the talent so he wouldn't lose it! The master got all of his money back. Why is he being so harsh?

But Jesus puts the matter in proper perspective with these words: "For everyone who has will be given more, and he will have an abundance. Whoever does not have, even what he has will be taken from him." The basic purpose of life is growth, increase, return. To fail in this purpose is to be unprofitable. The master has no use for servants who merely maintain the status quo, for they are unprofitable servants.

Many people who profess to be Christians are perfectly content to bury the opportunities God gives them. They are content with a stagnant life. They risk nothing, they gain nothing. All such people are unprofitable to God. Our Lord is in the investment business, and He intends to reap an increase from His investments.

The unprofitable servant had one opportunity to prove himself profitable, and he blew it. The outcome of the story tells us the nature of that opportunity. It was the opportunity to give himself to God, the opportunity to be redeemed. That one supreme venture was available to him throughout the time that his master was absent.

But what did he do with his one-and-only opportunity? He threw it into a hole in the ground and covered it with dirt! When it was safely buried, he could forget it and go on about his life. It was nowhere in view, where it might serve as an unpleasant reminder of the master's expectations. Since the unprofitable servant took no risk for Christ's sake, he had no spiritual influence, no impact for eternal good. His life counted for nothing and exhibited no spiritual power. His was a life lived for self, and in the end, he lost everything, including his own soul.

When the master returned, the unprofitable servant had a well-rehearsed speech ready. The gist of his defense was this: "Master, I know you are an unreasonable man. You expect other people to do all the work while you take all the benefits. If people fail to meet your unreasonable expectations, you punish them without mercy. I was afraid of you. I was afraid to risk what you gave me, because if I lost it, you would really be angry with me when you returned. So I played it smart. I kept the talent in a safe place to make sure it wouldn't get lost—see? Here it is, safe and sound! You didn't lose a penny!"

The master does not debate the servant's characterization of him as a hard and unreasonable man. He accepts that appraisal and says, "You wicked, lazy servant! So you knew that I harvest where I have not sown and gather where I have not scattered seed?" The editors of the New International Version have correctly ended this statement with a question mark. The master is not agreeing with what the servant says. He is saying, in effect, "So that is your understanding of my character, is it? All right, then, out of your own mouth will I judge you. If that's what you think of me, then you ought to have known that you couldn't possibly please me by failing to get some kind of gain. In that case, you could have at least put the money in the bank and I would have had some interest on it when I returned."

Of course, the real problem is that the unprofitable servant had no intention of being the servant he pretended to be. The master's argument is that no matter what his opinion of his master was, whether accurate or distorted, a true servant would have acted in accord with his master's expectations. The unprofitable servant refused to do this. He ignored his master's wishes and went about his life as if he were not a servant at all. He served himself instead of his lord. So he was a phony, a hypocrite, pretending to be a servant when he was not.

In his selfishness and willful blindness, the wicked servant failed to realize that his one chance to become genuine was to risk himself and the talent his master had given him. Had he done so, like the other two servants, he would have gained. He would have been *changed*, for to venture is to be changed. To risk for Christ's sake is to be forever altered, converted, redeemed, and reborn.

That one talent is given to all who are drawn to follow Christ. They have the opportunity to risk themselves while yet relying upon God's Word. They can trust His redeeming grace, resting their hope for eternity upon Christ's work for them on the cross. Other opportunities for risk will be provided later by a sovereign and loving God—but without that one initial investment there is no true value to life.

As C. S. Lewis vividly puts it in *Mere Christianity*, "It may be hard for an egg to turn into a bird: it would be a jolly sight harder for it to learn to fly while remaining an egg. We are like eggs at present. And you cannot go on indefinitely being just an ordinary, decent egg. We must be hatched or go bad." Most of us are content to be eggs. We do not want to risk leaving the shell. But God's plan for us is that we learn to fly—and no bird ever learned to fly without risk.

So the message of Jesus in this parable is: Step out! Risk! Live dangerously! Take chances with your life and your possessions for His sake. Cling to your life, and you will surely lose it. But surrender yourself to His cause, and you will gain your life and more!

That is the way to find life. That is the way to watch for His coming. Having risked yourself to become a Christian, now risk yourself again and again as opportunities arise. As you risk everything you are and everything you have, don't forget to risk your heart! Don't just live dangerously—*love* dangerously! Love as Jesus loved. Love the unlovely and the unloving and the unlovable. To live for Christ is to love others with a daring, risk-taking, Christlike love.

Love is truly an investment—an investment that entails great risk of loss and great potential for gain. Again, I quote C. S. Lewis, this time from his classic work on Christian love, *The Four Loves*. "There is no safe investment," Lewis wrote. "To love at all is to be vulnerable. Love anything and your heart will certainly be wrung and possibly be broken. . . . The only place outside heaven where you can be perfectly safe from all the dangers and perturbations of love is hell."

Jesus gave up everything to love us and die for us. What are we willing to risk for Him? ◇

13

The Stunning Surprise

Matthew 25:31–46

This is the last chapter!

If you have sneaked ahead to read it out of order because you can't wait to find out how it all ends, go ahead, read it! But come back to this chapter again when you've finished the rest of the book. It will make much better sense to you then.

If you have been following along since the beginning of the book, you'll be eager to know how Jesus closes this prophetic talk with His disciples on the Mount of Olives. At this point, He suddenly drops the use of parables and returns to a simple narrative. Unlike the parables of the household, the ten virgins, and the talents, the closing section of the Olivet discourse is told not in parable but in straightforward language. The theme of this section is judgment. Jesus uses the vivid metaphor of "sheep" and "goats" to describe what that judgment will be like:

> "When the Son of Man comes in his glory, and all the angels with him, he will sit on his throne in heavenly glory. All the nations will be gathered before him, and he will separate the people one from another as a shepherd separates the sheep from the goats. He will put the sheep on his right and the goats on his left." (Matthew 25:31–33)

It is important for us to remember that these words were spoken as Jesus stood in the gathering dusk on the Mount of Olives, facing a tiny band of forsaken men, looking out over a city where the plans were already being laid for His arrest and execution. When Jesus said these words, His cause already seemed lost. The powers of darkness seemed triumphant, the shadow of the cross darkened His path, the crowds that had once followed Him were turning away, His friends were fearful and powerless—and one of them was plotting to betray Him.

But as Jesus surveyed the centuries ahead, He saw the light that was yet to come. Without a hint of uncertainty, He declared, "When the Son of Man comes in his glory, and all the angels with him, he will sit on his throne in heavenly glory. All the nations will be gathered before him."

This gathering of the nations is confusing to some people. Does this mean that people will be judged according to the deeds of their government? No. Those who appear before the judgment seat of Christ do not come as Englishmen or Americans or Chinese or Afghans. The Greek word translated "nations" is *ethnos*, which literally means "Gentiles" or "heathens." Jesus is describing the judgment of the Gentiles, the non-Jewish peoples of earth. They are people living on earth at the time of the manifestation of His presence in power and great glory.

At this time, Jesus—who at this point in the prophecy has become Judge over all the earth—does what no other figure in human history could ever do: He dissolves all national distinctions, unites all the nations as one, and sits over them as their sovereign Judge. The purpose of this judgment is to determine who shall enter the kingdom of God that the Son has come to establish. Examine the words of Jesus throughout the gospels and you will see that the great passion of His heart, expressed again and again, is to see the will of God done on earth as it is in heaven.

Here, Jesus will manifest Himself in power as a fulfillment of the ancient visions of the Old Testament prophets—a vision of a world in which the righteousness of God fills the earth as the waters fill the sea. Only the righteous will be allowed to enter this kingdom.

The Sheep and the Goats

The meaning of the Lord's choice of metaphor seems obvious. There can be no doubt what Jesus means by the sheep and the goats. It is important to note, however, that it is a judgment of sheep and goats, not sheep and wolves! Jesus is not selecting between people who are obviously bad and people who are obviously good. There is no division here between the opponents of the gospel and the believers in it. That separation is to be made in the very moment of the appearing of Jesus in power and glory. As the apostle Paul writes:

> God is just: He will pay back trouble to those who trouble you and give relief to you who are troubled, and to us as well. This will happen when the Lord Jesus is revealed from heaven in blazing fire with his powerful angels. He will punish those who do not know God and do not obey the gospel of our Lord Jesus. They will be punished with everlasting destruction and shut out from the presence of the Lord and from the majesty of his power. (2 Thessalonians 1:6–9)

But the judgment of the sheep and the goats is a different judgment from the one Paul describes. In the judgment of the sheep and goats, Jesus culls the true and false from among all of those who profess to be Christians and claim to belong to Him as members of the family of God. It is the separation of the hypocrites from the real, of the false from the true.

Some commentators suggest (and I am inclined to agree) that there are *three* groups in this judgment scene: the sheep, the goats, and another group whom Jesus calls "these brothers of mine" (or "my brethren" in the King James Version). Here is what Jesus says:

> "Then the King will say to those on his right, 'Come, you who are blessed by my Father; take your inheritance, the kingdom prepared for you since the creation of the world. For I was hungry and you gave me something to eat, I was thirsty and you gave me something to drink, I was a stranger and you invited me in, I needed clothes and you clothed me, I was sick and you looked after me, I was in prison and you came to visit me.'
>
> "Then the righteous will answer him, 'Lord, when did we see you hungry and feed you, or thirsty and give you something to drink? When did we see you a stranger and invite you in, or needing clothes and clothe you? When did we see you sick or in prison and go to visit you?'
>
> "The King will reply, 'I tell you the truth, whatever you did for one of the least of these brothers of mine, you did for me.'" (Matthew 25:34–40)

These "brothers" of Jesus are Jewish people who have been undergoing a time of extreme trial and testing that involves hunger and thirst, homelessness and lack of adequate clothing, sickness and imprisonment. Clearly, this extreme level of suffering speaks of intense persecution. These "brothers" of Jesus, then, must be the 144,000 Jewish believers who are closely identified with the Lord during the whole period of His presence behind the scenes of the Great Tribulation.

In Isaiah 53:3, Jesus is prophetically described as "despised and rejected by men." We know that, during the Tribulation, these 144,000 Jewish Christians will also be despised and rejected, just as Jesus was. Anyone who shows kindness to these hated, hunted Jewish Christians in the last days will be taking an enormous risk and demonstrating a profound depth of love and kindness. Anyone caught ministering to the needs of those brothers and sisters of the Lord will immediately become the object of the fury and wrath of the Antichrist and his evil one-world government.

The Lord Jesus says to both the sheep and the goats, "whatever you did for one of the least of these brothers of mine, you did for me." That means, if you have shown kindness to the brothers of Jesus, you have shown kindness to Jesus Himself. If you have shown unkindness or indifference to the suffering, persecuted Jews, then it is as if you were unkind or indifferent toward Jesus Himself. All of this will be taken into account in the judgment of the sheep and the goats.

There are some Bible commentators who feel that the phrase "these brothers of mine" (or "my brethren") simply refers to any individual, Jewish or non-Jewish, who is in need in the last days. Still others would say that this phrase has universal application to both Jewish and non-Jewish people, whether in the present age or at the end of the age. But even if Jesus is speaking specifically of Jews during the Tribulation when He talks about "these brothers of mine," we still have a Christian obligation to show love and kindness to *all* people at *all* times. There can be no doubt that this principle remains in force now and for all time: If you show Christlike love to people in dire need, it is accounted as if you have shown love to Christ.

Whichever view you choose to hold, this much is certain: The principles of our Lord's judgment in the last days are no different from the principles by which He has judged human lives down through the centuries. As in the words of the "Gloria Patri," God's character is eternal and unchanging—"as it was in the beginning, is now, and ever shall be, world without end. Amen." The God of Genesis is the God of Revelation and of every book in between. His judgments are consistent from age to age. He will judge the hypocrites from among us today on the very same basis that He has judged them in all previous ages of history.

The Real Test

The arresting thing about the Lord's message at the close of His discourse is that He clearly states the ultimate mark of an authentic Christian. It is not his creed, his doctrine, or his Bible knowledge. It is the reality of his heart. It is the Christlike love and concern he shows to those who are in need. The practical demonstration of love is the final proof. The most orthodox Christian of all is the one who demonstrates an orthodoxy of love.

At this judgment Jesus does not ask anyone to present his case or argue his defense. He asks no questions. He examines no evidence. As judicial processes go, it is a brief and simple proceeding. He simply says to one group—the sheep—"Come, you who are blessed by my Father; take your inheritance, the kingdom prepared for you since the creation of the world."

Then Jesus explains the basis of His choice: When the sheep had an opportunity to help someone in need, they did it. Nothing more is required. It is sobering to realize that Jesus identifies Himself with those in need. "If you help people in need," Jesus says, in effect, "you are really helping Me. And if you ignore them, you ignore Me." Jesus flings the cloak of relationship around the needy and identifies with them as "brothers."

The sheep who inherit the kingdom are those who have responded to the needs of others. We may protest, "But it's costly and expensive to meet the needs of others." Or, "It's risky and dangerous to meet the needs of others." Well, yes, it is costly and risky to reach out in love to needy people. Jesus paid that price and took that risk every day of His public ministry. If we call ourselves "Christians," shouldn't we be willing to pay the price and take the risk to follow His example?

Those who live lives of costly, risky love receive a profound blessing from the Lord: entrance into the kingdom that was prepared before the foundation of the world. But what of those who refuse to pay the price and take the risk? What of those who have shown no love to the needy? They are the people Jesus symbolizes as "goats." To the goats, He says:

> "Depart from me, you who are cursed, into the eternal fire prepared for the devil and his angels. For I was hungry and you gave me nothing to eat, I was thirsty and you gave me nothing to drink, I was a stranger and you did not invite me in, I needed clothes and you did not clothe me, I was sick and in prison and you did not look after me.'" (Matthew 25:41–43)

We dare not ignore the severity of the Lord's words. "Depart from me, you who are cursed, into the eternal fire prepared for the devil and his angels." Remember, He is talking to people who thought all along that they were sheep! Imagine their astonishment to find that they are goats! No doubt, these people can point with pride to a moment when they made a profession of faith. They are probably quite dogmatic about biblical doctrines and creeds. They are church members in good standing—perhaps even leaders among the congregation.

But when they had the opportunity to help people in need, they shut their hearts and looked the other way. They paid no price, took no risk to reach out to the hungry, the thirsty, the homeless and ill-clothed, the sick and the imprisoned. They closed their ears to pleas for help. By their lack of love and compassion, they revealed themselves to be what they are: not sheep, but goats.

What a Surprise!

Both the sheep and the goats react to the Lord's words with stunned surprise. They are completely taken aback by what He says. It is evident that both groups expected a different basis for judgment. As they were being divided into one group or the other, they probably felt that the basis for the Lord's judgment would be "faith"—for, of course, the good news of Scripture is that we are justified before God by grace through faith.

Unfortunately, many people have the mistaken notion that "faith" means to give mental assent to a creed or doctrine—to say, "Yes, I believe in the Virgin Birth. I believe that Jesus is the Son of God, that He died on the cross to save me, and that He rose again from the dead." Those are important doctrines, but agreeing with a doctrine or creed is not faith.

Faith means to place complete trust in God, and to make a commitment of one's life to Jesus as Lord. Authentic conversion to Christ doesn't mean merely to adopt a set of beliefs; it means a complete transformation of life, a complete change of masters, and the adoption of the role of a servant to the One who is Lord of all.

No doubt there are many goats who have all the right beliefs but lack *faith*. They have tried to receive Jesus as Savior without also receiving Him as Lord. So, on the day of the judgment of the sheep and the goats, they stand and await their turn to face the King and Judge of all. Perhaps as they wait, each one nervously reviews his or her Christian testimony, trying to remember the promises of the Gospel in order to be prepared to make a defense for his or her soul. They recall the date that they made a profession of "faith," and perhaps they recall the very words of the prayer they prayed. They plan to offer that profession as Exhibit A in their own defense.

But this judgment is not a court trial. There is no prosecution, no defense, no time to present witnesses or evidence, no closing arguments, no objections. This judgment takes place before a sovereign Judge who knows all things. Those who stand trial before that Judge are not given a chance to say a word in their defense. The verdict and the sentence are instantly rendered, case closed. Each person is simply told to which group he or she belongs—the sheep or the goats.

The sheep are asked to take their place on the right hand of the throne, because their genuine faith has produced a lifetime of good works. Their good works cannot save them, but their good works prove the genuineness of their faith. Without a thought of reward, these authentic Christians have quietly lived out the example of their Lord, responding to the pleas and needs of the people around them. They have kept no records, they have expected no praise. They were unaware they were doing anything unusual. It was simply their joy and privilege to minister to others in Christ's name.

But not one loving deed has escaped the eye of their watching Lord. He does not need to examine them. He knows them and their deeds. They are His sheep, and they have laid up abundant treasure in heaven. The sheep are surprised to hear that what they did for others they did for Jesus. They had no idea that in serving others, they were truly ministering to Him.

But the goats are equally surprised. They, too, are caught off guard by the basis of the Lord's judgment. Jesus goes on to say:

> "They also will answer, 'Lord, when did we see you hungry or thirsty or a stranger or needing clothes or sick or in prison, and did not help you?' (Matthew 25:44)

These goats know that God is interested in the poor, the downtrodden, the oppressed. They may have made long mental lists of the many times they have ministered to people in need. They can produce itemized records of the money they have contributed, complete with income tax receipts. Among the goats will be people who have spent much of their lives working for charity, fighting for racial equality, and protesting substandard housing—but they did it for their own glory, not His. To these self-justifying, self-righteous goats, Jesus has a scathing response:

> "He will reply, 'I tell you the truth, whatever you did not do for one of the least of these, you did not do for me.'
> "Then they will go away to eternal punishment, but the righteous to eternal life." (Matthew 25:45–46)

The goats are even more surprised than the sheep at the Lord's words. They have been depending on good deeds to gain acceptance into the kingdom. They are at a total loss to understand the Lord's rejection. But they have forgotten what Jesus said in the Sermon on the Mount:

> "Be careful not to do your 'acts of righteousness' before men, to be seen by them. If you do, you will have no reward from your Father in heaven.

"So when you give to the needy, do not announce it with trumpets, as the hypocrites do in the synagogues and on the streets, to be honored by men. I tell you the truth, they have received their reward in full. But when you give to the needy, do not let your left hand know what your right hand is doing, so that your giving may be in secret. Then your Father, who sees what is done in secret, will reward you." (Matthew 6:1–4)

When it comes to good works, our motivation matters. Those who do good works just to get noticed and praised already have their reward. Those who do good works out of a love for others and a desire to please God will get their reward in the kingdom that was prepared before the foundation of the world. Not only should we not seek praise and notice from others when we do good works—we should not even take any note of it ourselves. We should not let our left hand know what our right hand is doing. In other words, we should not even privately pat ourselves on the back!

The Difference Between Our Judgment and God's

The goats remember the good deeds they did with the motive of pumping up their reputation or their spiritual pride. But Jesus takes no notice of the deeds the goats remember, because the goats already have their reward for those deeds. What Jesus remembers is all the opportunities for ministry the goats have had, but have failed to seize. Jesus remembers the times they stepped over a beggar on the sidewalk, the times they ignored the sick and the dying because they were just too busy, the times when pride and self-righteousness prevented them from visiting some poor wretch in prison. Jesus remembers the times these goats averted their eyes from someone's pain or shut their ears to someone's plea.

The goats remember no such incidents. Their lost opportunities for ministry have been long forgotten. They are honestly astonished when they ask Jesus, "When did we see you in need and fail to help you?" They did not notice at the time, so they do not remember when it is time for judgment.

No doubt, many of these goats have called themselves evangelical Christians. But the goats have practiced a false Christianity, no matter how much it may be dressed in evangelical clothes.

Perhaps nothing describes the goat's mindset better than this prayer, written by Richard Woike. He calls it "A Prayer to Avoid," but we might well call it "The Prayer of a Goat."

> O thou pleasant, comfortable, kindly, good-natured God: How glad I am that I can look forward, with a reasonable degree of certainty, to another ordinary day. Keep me today from anything that taxes my faith, from discomfort, from unnecessary strain, from unusual problems, especially those involving sickness or death, or the necessity of extending financial aid to relatives and friends.

> Dear Lord, grant that nothing may occur which will disturb my satisfaction with the way I am, and the things I say, and the thoughts I think, the acts I do, or the many deeds I leave undone. Give me this day, in addition to my daily bread, the butter, meats, and sweetmeats that are my necessary diet, and let me not be troubled by qualms of conscience concerning the amount of time and money I spend on food and clothing, pastimes, good and bad, and those pursuits which, while not of spiritual value, are the accepted hallmark of the normal citizen of this enlightened community in this enlightened age.

> About the future and the darkening trend of things, keep me from thoughtfulness. Events rush on, the world travails.

Can screaming headlines prove thy hand's at work this very
moment, bringing near that fateful cry, 'Behold! He comes!'?
O, Lord, such disconcerting thoughts! Keep me from worry-
ing about such things, and guide me safely to and from my
office, and my home. Amen."

Nothing reveals more clearly the radical difference between
God's judgment and human judgment than this story of the sheep
and the goats. The brilliant, white-hot light of God's throne shows
up our most treasured "good deeds" for what they really are. Good
deeds that come from selfish motives rather than from genuine love
are not good deeds at all! They are planned performances, contrived
acts, dishonest poses. They are an attempt to *purchase* God's favor
through our own self-righteous work.

God's judgment takes note only of the unselfconscious
moments of our lives—the times when we are behaving authenti-
cally and honestly, when we reveal our true selves. As David told his
son Solomon in 1 Chronicles 28:9, "The LORD searches every heart
and understands every motive behind the thoughts."

This truth was impressed upon me when I attended a concert
with friends in a large city. Officials of the city and state were in
attendance, along with a crowd of people who jammed a small
open-air square. The officials were seated in front-row chairs on a
small platform. Among the performers was a young starlet from
Hollywood. She was skimpily dressed in a strapless evening gown.
She performed several lively songs, swaying her hips and snapping
her fingers.

As she sang, I noticed the reaction of the mayor, who sat in the
first row. To put it politely, you could see in his face exactly what
was on his mind. I also saw the governor of the state, a few chairs
away, watching the mayor with obvious disapproval. The governor

caught the mayor's eye, and the mayor discovered he was being observed. The mayor reddened, shifted in his chair, closed his mouth, and sat up straight. Without a word being exchanged, I had just seen a message of incomparable eloquence conveyed from the governor to the mayor: "Shape up, man! Set an example! People are watching you!" The mayor was the model of propriety throughout the rest of the evening—but the motives of his heart had been exposed.

Our lives will not be judged on the basis of those times when we are consciously on our best behavior, those times when we are being extra-careful not to get "caught." Our lives will be judged on the basis of what we do when we think no one is watching, when we are, as the old *Candid Camera* show used to put it, "caught in the act of being ourselves."

Does that mean God expects us to never fail? No, we will fail, and He knows that. But He does expect us to build Christ into our lives on a daily, hourly, moment-by-moment basis. There is only one kind of life that can transform us from goats into sheep, and that is the life of the Shepherd Himself. Only *He* is capable of responding to human need with risky, unselfish love. Only *He* is capable of doing good deeds out of pure and unsullied motives— so we must build His life into our lives.

If we have not received Him into our hearts, we do not have His life in our lives. Once we have received Him, we need to make ourselves available to Him. We must invite Him to live through us as He brings opportunities for love and ministry our way. We must be willing to set aside our agendas and schedules and wants and wishes in order to reach out to others in the strength and love He imparts to us.

This alone is the life that meets the test. This alone is the life of a true sheep, led by the Great Shepherd.

The One Great Word—Watch!

Now the Olivet discourse is ended. We have heard the greatest Prophet who ever lived outline for us the history of the future. It has been a fascinating experience, containing many surprising and unexpected revelations. If we had never read this discourse before, we could not possibly have guessed the outcome of human history.

Now we know the end of the story. But now that we know, what will we do about it? What will our response be?

There can be only one answer to that question, the same answer that our Lord has given us: *Watch!* The issue of watchfulness and readiness is so important to the Lord that He underscores it four times throughout the Olivet discourse:

Matthew 24:4—"*Watch out* that no one deceives you."

Matthew 24:42—"Therefore *keep watch*, because you do not know on what day your Lord will come."

Matthew 24:44—"So you also must *be ready*, because the Son of Man will come at an hour when you do not expect him."

Matthew 25:13—"Therefore *keep watch*, because you do not know the day or the hour."

Watch out! Be ready! Keep watch! Having worked our way through the entire Olivet discourse, we now understand what it means to watch. The meaning of this command can be summed up in three specific principles:

1. To *watch* means to help one another feed upon the living Lord Jesus, as He is revealed in the written Word of God. We must study the Bible.

2. To *watch* means to walk in the Spirit, depending not upon our fallible human resources but upon the power of God's indwelling Spirit at work in us.

3. To *watch* means we must live dangerously, venturing and risking for Christ's sake. We must boldly take advantage of every opportunity to meet the needs of those around us, with no thought of reward or praise.

As Jesus says in Luke's gospel, "Be always on the watch, and pray that you may be able to escape all that is about to happen, and that you may be able to stand before the Son of Man" (Luke 21:36).

This is what it means to watch and wait for the Lord's return.

THE END

End Notes

1. Editors' Note: The author here introduces an idea based on the fact that the term *parousia,* translated "coming" in Matthew 24:3, 27, 37, 39, encompasses the idea of an abiding presence. Most Bible teachers do not hold to the view that Jesus will appear and disappear repeatedly during the interval between His coming for the church and His return to establish the Messianic kingdom.

2. Editors' Note: In 2 Thessalonians 2:8, *epiphania* describes the return of Christ as King, but the term also refers to the coming of Jesus for His church (the Rapture) as in 1 Timothy 6:14; 2 Timothy 4:8; and Titus 2:13. Premillenial Bible teachers generally hold that the context must determine the exact meaning of the terms *parousia* and *epiphania.*